Nature, the Artful Modeler

THE PAUL CARUS LECTURES

PUBLISHED IN MEMORY OF

PAUL CARUS
1852–1919

Editor of
The Open Court
and
The Monist
from
1888 to 1919

The Paul Carus Lecture Series 23

Nature, the Artful Modeler

Lectures on Laws, Science, How Nature Arranges the World and How We Can Arrange It Better

Nancy Cartwright

OPEN COURT
Chicago

THE PAUL CARUS LECTURE SERIES 23

To find out more about Open Court books, call toll-free 1-9-800-815-2280 or visit our website at www.opencourtbooks.com.

Open Court Publishing Company is a division of Carus Publishing Company, dba Cricket Media.

Copyright © 2019 by Carus Publishing Company, dba Cricket Media

First printing 2019

All rights reserved. No part of this publication may be reproduced, stored in a retrieval system, or transmitted, in any form or by any means, electronic, mechanical, photocopying, recording, or otherwise, without the prior written permission of the publisher, Open Court Publishing Company, 70 East Lake Street, Suite 800, Chicago, Illinois 60601.

Printed and bound in the United States of America.

Nature, the Artful Modeler: Lectures on Laws, Science, How Nature Arranges the World and How We Can Arrange It Better

ISBN: 978-0-8126-9468-0

Library of Congress Control Number: 2019930416
This book is also available as an e-book (ISBN 978-0-8126-9472-7)

These lectures are dedicated to Vivian Weil, who (in the words of John Douard) turned engineering into a profession by giving it an ethics, and on account of whom I have always wanted to be better.

Nature, the Artful Modeler: She Reads *The New Yorker*, Trusts in God, and Takes Short Views.

Contents

Preface ix
Acknowledgments xi

PART 1
THE CARUS LECTURES 1

1. Nature's Methods Are Our Methods
That's why ours work so well. But she is not Kant, the grand synthesizer; Augustus Caesar, whose decrees went out to all the world; nor Boole, Frege, Russell, or Peano, doyens of deduction. Perhaps Isambard Brunel, with his dockyards, railways, and steamships; Margaret Knight, whose machines made flat-bottomed paper bags, cut shoe soles, and raised sash windows; or Alice Waters, creator of super new California cuisines. 3

2. Nature's Raw Materials
Powers, arrangements, and causes. She manages actual possibilities, obeys the Barcan formula, and does not sit down with counterfactuals. 29

3. Nature's Limits
Picking up where Nature leaves off, building it better, and warranting your work. 55

Afterword
Richard Vagnino 77

Part 2
Further Thoughts on Contingency and Order — 79

4. Is the Cat Really Lapping Up the Milk? — 81

5. Big Systems versus Stocky Tangles: It Can Matter to the Details — 101

6. Are Laws of Nature Consistent with Contingency?
   Nancy Cartwright and Pedro Merlussi — 111

7. The Natural and the Moral Order: What's to Blame — 117

References — 147
Index — 155

Preface: What's Here?

This book contains my three 2017 Carus lectures (chapters 1 through 3), plus four further papers that develop and support the central theses of the Carus lectures: that a very great deal of our important scientific knowledge is knowledge-how not knowledge-that; that, concomitantly, many of our most useful principles (including high-level 'laws' of physics) are neither true nor false but are rather (in the words of Pierre Duhem) 'symbolic representations' that we use to model, predict, and navigate the world; that a good many of these symbolic representations are short-hand labels for powers and our practices for using them; that our scientific successes do not suggest that Nature operates by 'law' in fixing what happens; rather the world is full of possibilities and what happens is best recouped by artful modeling.

Chapters 4 and 5 defend my claims that possibilities are real. This is of course a huge philosophical issue. I stick to the philosophy of science side of it, in dialogue with two giants in philosophy of science, both great defenders of the opposing view that possibility, indeed all modality, is only in the model—in our representations of the world—and not in the world itself: Wolfgang Spohn and Bas van Fraassen. The discussion with Spohn was in celebration in 2015 of his Frege Prize and with van Fraassen at a special event organized for this purpose by the Philosophy Department at UC Davis and the (San Francisco) Bay Area Philosophy of Science group in 2018.

The theme of modality with respect to the 'laws of nature' is pursued in depth in the joint work with Pedro Merlussi in chapter 6. How much contingency do these allow under various philosophic understandings of them: on a Mill-Ramsey-Lewis 'Humean' systematizing-regularities view, or if they are seen as relations between universals, or as having to do with powers? The issue is not just 'Do they govern' but other questions about their modal reach: 'What do they cover? What do they insist should happen and what is permitted? Can they have exceptions and still 'hold'? On inspection it seems as if these issues are for the most part orthogonal to what a law is taken to be. In particular, contrary to a common expectation, accounts that focus on powers do not fit or fail to fit with contingency any more readily than the other accounts.

My third Carus lecture—chapter 3 here—was practically focused: How we can use our scientific know-how about powers and their activities to improve on what is happening naturally in the world, or as a result of the social, economic, political, and cultural structures that are already in place? A major theme is the importance of structures—the *arrangements* of powers that affects what happens when they act in consort. This echoes the slogan often repeated nowadays in policy deliberation: 'Context matters.' Chapter 7 develops this theme further, in particular looking at how the moral and the natural order interweave when different concepts of causality support different loci for blame and responsibility. This chapter first appeared in a volume in honor of the historian of science Lorraine Daston. It was inspired by her brilliant and imaginative Tanner Lectures on Human Values at Harvard University in 2002, "The Moral Authority of Nature."

Nancy Cartwright
January 2019

Acknowledgments

The thinking behind these lectures and the additional papers included here has been influenced by myriad conversations and work with students, teachers, colleagues, friends, and adversaries over decades. I would like to thank them all for the immense help they have been. It has also been supported by the universities at which I have worked and visited and by a number of generous grants from private and public bodies, for which I am also extremely grateful.

Besides Durham University and the University of California at San Diego, work for this book was supported by the Templeton-funded LSE/UCSD project, *God's Order, Man's Order and the Order of Nature* and by the Durham project *Knowledge for Use* (*K4U*), which has received funding from the European Research Council (ERC) under the European Union's Horizon 2020 research and innovation program (grant agreement No 667526 K4U). The content reflects only the author's view and the ERC is not responsible for any use that may be made of the information it contains.

The epigraph is a reference to W. H. Auden's Hermetic Decalogue (from "Under Which Lyre"). I hope that my work here can be excused for committing a social science.

Figure 1.2 (design for Millikan's experiment) is reprinted with permission from Allan Franklin, "Millikan's Oil-Drop Experiments," *Chem. Educator* 2, no. 1 (1997). Copyright 2019 by the American Physical Society.

Figure 1.3 (photo of Millikan's apparatus) is reprinted courtesy of the Archives, California Institute of Technology.

Figure 1.4 (Nature Conservancy model for a marine reserve) is reprinted with permission from: TNC, 2007. *Conservation Action Planning Handbook: Developing Strategies, Taking Action and Measuring Success at Any Scale*. The Nature Conservancy, Arlington, VA.

Figure 3.2 is reprinted from *What Works in Conservation*, W. J. Sutherland, L.V. Dicks, N. Ockendon, and R. K. Smith (Cambridge, UK: Open Book Publishers, 2015). http://dx.doi.org/10.11647/OBP.0060

Chapter 5, "Big Systems versus Stocky Tangles: It Can Matter to the Details" is reprinted from *Erkenntnis* 2017.

Chapter 6, "Are Laws of Nature Consistent with Contingency?," N. Cartwright and P. Merlussi, originally appeared in *Laws of Nature*, edited by W. Ott and L. Patto, 221–44 (Oxford: Oxford University Press, 2018). Reproduced with permission of the Licensor through PLSclear.

Chapter 7, "The Natural and the Moral Order: What's to Blame?", is reprinted from Wendy Doniger, Peter Galison, and Susan Neiman, eds., *What Reason Promises: Essays on Reason, Nature and History*, Berlin, Boston: De Gruyter, 2016, 13–18.

PART 1

The Carus Lectures

1

Nature's Methods Are Our Methods

... That's why ours work so well. But she is not Kant, the grand synthesizer; Augustus Caesar, whose decrees went out to all the world; nor Boole, Frege, Russell, or Peano, doyens of deduction. Perhaps Isambard Brunel, with his dockyards, railways, and steamships; Margaret Knight, whose machines made flat-bottomed paper bags, cut shoe soles, and raised sash windows, or Alice Waters, creator of super new California cuisines.

INTRODUCTION

These lectures aim to show that, when it comes to fixing what comes to pass, Nature is an artful modeler. What then is an 'artful modeler'? We have a paradigm in our own methods for designing the phenomenal devices we use to make our lives easier, more fun, safer, and more rewarding: the Oxford knee, the gyroscopes for the Stanford gravity probe, the successful evacuation of 88,000 people from the massive forest fire at Fort McMurray, Alberta, wartime radar, or the new extra-quiet, energy-saving dishwashers.

The sources of knowledge that go into any one of these designs are many, and varied, crossing the boundaries of natural and social science, engineering, technology, and everyday life. They may include, in one fell swoop, equations and principles of fundamental theory, from physics to cell biology to game theory; rough and ready precepts, often very context and subject specific; and an understanding of materials and people and how they are wont to behave—what they can be relied on for, what not, and what they might be able to do.

The art is in:

- Figuring out what knowledge to call on
- Understanding what can be done with that knowledge
- Bringing the nuggets of different kinds of knowledge together into a coherent model to produce accurate predictions.

There are some reliable general rules we can call on to help (like vector addition of forces), many rules of thumb (don't tell the other committee members they're jerks if you want to win the vote) and many *ceteris paribus* rules (generally, each crystalline substance has a single characteristic crystallographic form), and much defeasible advice (try shutting down the computer and restarting). But these are rarely enough to draft a model or to fix what to expect when the device is assembled. Designing a device is *artful*: It cannot be done by the book. Although I introduce the idea by pointing to human inventions, artfulness is equally—or probably even more—prominent in the models we use to generate reliable predictions about complicated situations we do not design.

My central thesis is familiar from Democritus onwards: Technology learns from and *imitates* Nature—but decidedly without the Aristotelian twist. In addition to Plato's pragmatic distinction between knowledge of unchanging things versus opinion of changing things, we know that Aristotle distinguished *techné*, 'craft' or 'art', from *episteme*, 'genuine knowledge',[1] which is the domain of pure theory. We also know he thought that genuine knowledge is of necessary and unchanging truths, like those of geometry. I shall argue that, if theory is in the business of truth—unchanging or otherwise, then it won't have much business to do. This follows from a more fundamental disagreement with the Aristotelian point of view, which is my overall theme in these lectures. Aristotle (and Plato even more so) viewed *techné* as an imperfect human representation of Nature. I propose this

> Central thesis: *Techné* provides the very best representations
> of Nature that are possible, human or otherwise—because
> this is just what Nature is like.

This is not a pragmatic theory of truth nor a point about the nature and limits of human understanding, as we might read Habermas, Gadamer,

---

[1] And the closely related 'wisdom' (*sofia*) and 'intuition' (*nous*). Juan Carlos Gonzalez suggests that one might say that nature as artful modeler has *phronesis*, or practical wisdom, because *phronesis* incorporates both deliberation and skillful coping or expertise.

or Rorty. Rather, it is an ontological thesis. *Techné* can embody genuine knowledge, it need not be an *imperfect* human representation, because Nature does it the way we do. Nature fixes what happens in the way that we predict it. She, like us, is an artful modeler.

What is the alternative? There are three immediately obvious proposals:

- Nature is a rule follower. She does it by the book.
- Nature is a creature of habit. She does in each new situation what she did in situations like that before.
- Nature is capricious. She has no strategy for deciding what comes next.

I think there is too much order in the world to endorse the third. It also seems to make our own successes at prediction and control mysterious: How do we manage to predict what happens if there is no rhyme nor reason to it? I shall thus not discuss this alternative further.

It has been a longstanding view of mine that the second is not correct either, at least for the most part. Nature seldom confronts just the same situation all over again. This is why John Stuart Mill thought that economics cannot be an inductive science.[2] The arrangements of causes that act together to produce what happens are not stable. They shift about, and when they do so what has happened in the past, even if it has been duplicated for a while, cannot be relied on to hold in the future. This is true in general. Nature continually faces new situations with new arrangements, the ones we invent not the least of these, and she needs to decide what to do where habit will not dictate.

I shall argue that the possibilities for new arrangements are endless, and they don't fall into articulable categories. This makes real troubles for the remaining alternative: Nature is a rule follower. But I want to start with *us* before moving on to Nature. Our modern sciences do not apply to the world 'by the book'. We do not predict and manage the world by tracing out the consequences of scientific laws, but by situation-specific models; and there are no fixed rules for how to build these models nor for how to evaluate their reliability. Our scientific understanding of the world is not, then, in knowledge-that but in knowledge-how.

Nor could it be in knowledge-that since much of what we label 'scientific principle' is not well-formulated enough to count as a claim to begin with, let alone one that is somewhere in the ballpark of true. I shall argue

---

[2] Mill 1948.

this in Section 1, but it is witnessed by the repeated failures of attempts by me and others to turn our scientific principles into propositions that could plausibly be true.

The insight that this whole enterprise is a mistake is inspired by Hasok Chang's brilliant new work on 'Active Scientific Knowledge'.[3] (It also resonates with Andrea Woody's functional perspective on scientific explanations.[4]) Chang sees scientific knowledge as the ability to carry out epistemic activities successfully. Both he and I start from a longstanding focus on practice. Chang aims to reconceive scientific truth as "pragmatist coherence." I urge we give up on truth altogether for much of what gets labeled 'scientific principle'. Not that these principles are false. Rather they are not candidates for truth or falsehood. This should not be a surprise. Most of them, as they come, are not well-formed formulae; they don't express propositions. Nor do we use them as such. We use them, often in the exact form we find in textbooks and research reports, as pieces in a model to construct empirical claims about real embodied systems that can be judged of their truth and falsehood. Based on similar observations, Pierre Duhem called the laws of physics "symbolic representations."[5] I shall follow him in that: a good number of our most useful scientific principles do not make claims at all. They are mere symbolic representations. In Section 2 I shall show how this claim can reconfigure the scientific realism debate.

Perhaps it is not so disturbing that we are not logic choppers but rather artful modelers; it may even be thought a more attractive self-image. But Nature too, I urge, is an artful modeler. Why? First, that's what empiricism dictates. If our successful predictions about Nature's outcomes are not derivable from law claims, what evidence is there that Nature's outcomes themselves derive from laws? I shall pursue this line of argument in Section 2 when I turn to scientific realism. Section 1 shows why Nature cannot fix what comes to pass in accord with well-formulated law claims.

Lecture 2 explores the way Nature uses powers when she engineers what happens and defends what Florian Fischer has labeled a *Trias* account of powers. Lecture 3 is an exercise in the philosophy of social technology. It puts all this to practical use in figuring out how to make reliable predictions about the effectiveness of our social policies.

---

[3] Chang Forthcoming.
[4] Woody 2015.
[5] Duhem 1991.

1. Why We Must Be Artful Modelers

I maintain that our scientific successes come not by derivation from principles but by artful modeling.[6] Our scientific understanding of the world is not, then, in knowledge-that but in knowledge-how. We are inclined to think that this is not so in physics and, really, it's all physics anyway. So I start with physics. But I do not want to remain there because so much of the modeling we do—and that Nature must do—uses hardly any physics at all.[7] I shall offer three arguments as to why both we, and Nature, must be artful modelers. The first involves the relations among features located in different disciplines and at different 'levels'.[8] The second has to do with how things act in combination. The third has to do with powers and their contributions, which I delay till Lecture 2.

1. i Getting Different Domains Together

1. i a The Millikan experiment: What Millikan had to do[9]

Physics is the beau ideal of exact science. It lays down precise principles among well-characterized concepts. It is also, as Popper urged, falsifiable. Falsifiability is ultimately not a matter of principle but of practice, and practice often not in the hands of physicists, but of engineers and technicians. Here, I shall argue, Nature, like us, must be an artful modeler.

Consider the famous 1909 oil drop experiment of Robert Millikan, with the aid of Harvey Fletcher, to measure the charge of the electron, pictured in Figure 1.1.

---

[6] This is a view I share with Mauricio Suarez, who claims, for instance, "Some models of the phenomena cannot be embedded in any theory, not even in those theories employed to build the models in the first place. Some examples include gravitational lensing models in cosmology, stellar structure models in astrophysics and models of SQUIDS (superconducting quantum interference devices)" (p. 52) and "Phenomena that the theory successfully gets applied to can be neither reduced to, nor embedded in, the theory" (p. 57). For Suarez's arguments for this view, see Suarez 2005.

[7] Or perhaps I should say "deep physics" to contrast with things like the law of the lever, which we certainly use in a great many technological devices, from the toaster to the Oxford knee.

[8] I use scare quotes because I, like many others, do not think we can in the end make much of this idea of levels. See for example, Mariam Thalos's *Without Hierarchy* (Thalos 2013) or Helen Longino's *Studying Human Behavior: How Scientists Investigate Aggression and Sexuality* (Longino 2013).

[9] I am here following up on Florian Fischer's use of this example in his thesis, *Laws of Nature as Dispositions* (2018).

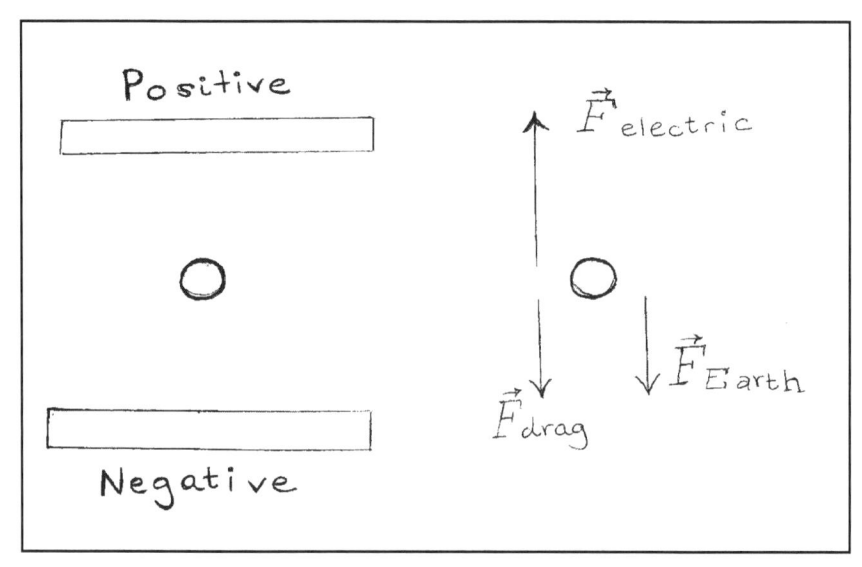

Figure 1.1 Millikan's Experiment, as Theorized. Drawing by Lucy Charlton.

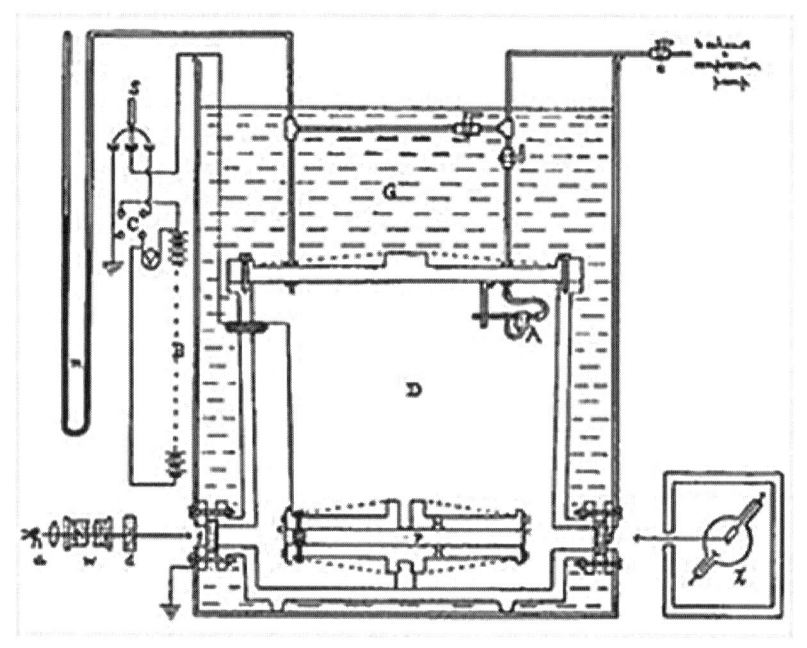

Figure 1.2 Design for Millikan's Experiment. Reprinted with permission from "Millikan's Oil-Drop Experiments," A. Franklin, *The Chem. Educator* 2, no. 1 (1997): 4.

A negatively charged oil droplet hovers between two charged plates, pulled down by gravity and up by electric attraction. Due to air resistance, it also feels a drag force proportional to its velocity. Millikan measured the charge q on the droplet by adjusting the electric field strength till the droplet was at rest, so he could calculate $F_{electric} = qE = F_{earth} \oplus F_{drag}$, where the two terms on the right, as well as the size of the electric field, E, are determined by a combination of theory and measurement. The charge q is due to free electrons on the oil drop, all of which have the same charge q_e. Though the drops differ in charge, for each drop, $q = nq_e$; so q_e can be estimated by measuring q for a number of drops.

Everything here looks 'by the book': in accord with general principles. But principle is not enough. The depiction in Figure 1.1 is just that, a depiction. Millikan needed to create the features depicted in Figure 1.1 in the world.

His design for how to do so is in Figure 1.2.

Figure 1.3 shows the actual embodiment of Figures 1.1 and 1.2 in his lab.

Here principle gives out and practice takes over. Consider this warning for the host of physics students who are expected to repeat Millikan's experiment but nowadays with fancy equipment made just for that task: "Students should also recognize, at the outset, the scientific, technological,

Figure 1.3 Millikan's Real Apparatus. Courtesy of the Archives, California Institute of Technology.

and methodological complexity of the oil drop experiment which made (*and still makes*) it difficult to obtain consistent and accurate results."[10]

Think for instance about what is simply labeled $F_{electric}$ in Figure 1.2. This is produced by a potential difference [P.D.] between the two plates. See what Millikan has to say about this seemingly simple quantity; notice how much art it took to embody a precise value of $F_{electric}$:

> The potential difference is not reliably given by the battery voltage. It is measured in 6 parts with a device accurate to 1 part in 2000. This device in turn is calibrated by a second, whose accuracy is both certified and independently measured by yet a third device. And 5000 readings calibrated in two different ways were shown to be consistent. The electric fields were produced by a 5,300-volt storage battery, the P.D. of which dropped on an average 5 or 10 volts during an observation of an hour's duration. The potential readings were taken, just before and just after a set of observations on a given drop, by dividing the bank into 6 parts and reading the P.D. of each part with a 900-volt Kelvin and White electrostatic voltmeter which showed remarkable constancy and could be read easily, in this part of the scale, with an accuracy of about 1 part in 2,000. This instrument was calibrated by comparison with a 750-volt Weston Laboratory Standard Voltmeter certified correct to 1/10 per cent, and actually found to have this accuracy by comparison with an instrument standardized at the Bureau of Standards in Washington. The readings of P.D. should therefore in no case contain an error of more than 1 part in 1,000. As a matter of fact 5,000 volt readings made with the aid of two different calibration curves of the K. 8c W instrument made two years apart never differed by more than 1 or 2 parts in 5,000.[11]

Millikan did not move from what's in Figure 1.1 to what's in Figure 1.3 'by the book'. If there'd been a book, his would not have been an experimental tour de force. When it comes to the embodiment of the theoretical concepts in Figure 1.1, principle leaves off and practice takes over. What I mean by "principle leaves off" for concepts like F_{drag} is this:

> There is no principle in physics[12] that says, for some well characterized descriptions D and M, 'When D, then T = M', where

---

[10] Klassen 2009, 601 (my emphasis).
[11] Millikan 1913, 112.
[12] I assume here that the principles in question should satisfy the five requirements laid out in Section 2.A.

T is filled in by the theoretical concept and M by a more concrete description of how that concept is materially instantiated given D.

Millikan needed to be an artful modeler.

1. i b Millikan's experiment: What Nature had to do

That's Millikan. What is Nature doing in Millikan's experiment? Note first that Nature's job is far more difficult than Millikan's. When Millikan builds his apparatus, he need only know that the materials and arrangements he chooses will embody the forces represented in Figure 1.1.[13] Millikan's models in Figures 1.1 and 1.2 represent only a tiny fraction of the features and behaviors of the device in Figure 1.3. Nature must fix everything there is about them. And she must do so in a way that leaves one consistent world with the happenings that we have succeeded in modeling in it.

Her job can be made to look easier. If the world were just one big mosaic of Humean features—say those that fundamental physics studies—and these could be summed up in deterministic laws, then all Nature need do is lay down the initial conditions and consult the laws to settle what should happen next. What though of all the other features? The oiliness of Millikan's oil, its smoke point, its color, its taste, its extremely low vapor pressure?[14] We know that this is a highly-debated topic in philosophy. Roughly the standard answers can be grouped into four basic viewpoints.

> 1. *These features are not really there.* They are an artifact of the set of mistaken concepts with which we approach the world. In what Wilfrid Sellars[15] called "the manifest image," which is constructed in terms of our mistaken concepts, the pink ice cube is pink through and through, quite contrary to what is 'really' the case.
>
> Whatever views like this have in favor and against them, they don't solve Nature's problem. Even if features corresponding to our manifest-image concepts are not really there, we still have a great deal of intersubjective agreement

---

[13] And no others that will make a significant difference to the drop's motion.
[14] Millikan used high-grade clock oil which should then have had a viscosity little affected by temperature change and with a low tendency to spread or evaporate (which is the reason Millikan, urged by Fletcher, switched from water drops, which evaporated too quickly, to oil) or to react adversely with air or metals. (These are the characteristics recommended for clock oils by the British Horological Institute, 2008.)
[15] Sellars 1962.

in their application. The oil feels oily to you as well as to me. Nature needs to affix this 'seeming oily'-ness to some bits of the Humean mosaic and not others.

2. *Type-type reductionism*. Our philosophical favorite is 'temperature in an ideal gas = mean kinetic energy of the molecules that compose the gas'. This alternative is out of fashion now, in philosophy of science because it turns out to be very difficult to find enough of these type-type correlations, and in more general philosophy, because of the doctrine of multiple realizability: 'higher level' features can be realized in many different configurations of the basic Humean features. That is a pity, though, for this is the one view that supposes there are *principles* that describe the association of features. Type-type reductionism pictures Nature as doing it by the book.

3. *Supervenience*. Once the base Humean features are fixed, all else is fixed, though not the reverse. As a philosopher of science, this view has always puzzled me. I can see why one might maintain that once the position and velocity of a particle is fixed, and the forces on it, so too is its motion. This can be seen to be what Newtonian physics says, and hence to be supported by a vast amount of empirical evidence. But where is the empirical evidence for any specific supervenience claim?

4. *Then there is my view*. Why suppose our theories, whether in fundamental particle physics, electrical engineering, or the sociology of the family, give us an understanding of the world? Because they allow us to manage and predict it, sometimes very precisely. But it is not theory that describes the real embodied systems that we manage; rather it is system-specific models. The models feature factors from different domains and different levels interacting in different ways. Micro features constrain and help cause macro ones, and the reverse. They work in teams across levels, constraining and causing each other.

The roles we assign the features in our models are not for the most part arbitrary; they are prompted by the principles from our mixed bag of theories. We may then find system-specific propositions to associate with those principles, perhaps like this one:

In Millikan's apparatus on xx date at xx time,
$\mathbf{F}_{drag}$ was approximately $6\pi\alpha\mu v/(1 + Al/\alpha)$.

These are proper propositions whose truth is evidenced in the success of the model. We can imagine then producing a description, say D, of the state of Millikan's apparatus at that time and endorsing a more general claim:

Whenever D, then $\mathbf{F}_{drag}$ is approximately $6\pi\alpha\mu v/(1 + Al/\alpha)$.

But it is important to keep in mind that context-specific generalizations like this are always defeasible by adding more to the description. So they must always include a *nothing-else rider* (NE) among their conditions:

NE: Nothing else obtains relevant to the outcome than the conditions described.

Suppose there were a non-context-dependent rendering of some particular principle for a set of features, F. The content of this non-context-dependent proposition, what it amounts to in a real concrete situation, would be supplied by context-dependent principles involving F; so too would be the evidence for its truth. So the context-dependent propositions must be instances of whatever non-context-dependent proposition is floated. But no matter what F is, there is an endless array of arrangements with other features that F can get itself into, and correlatively an endless array of context-dependent truths associated with the principle in question. *There are too many of these and they pull in too many directions to admit of one consistent proposition that covers them all.*

I imagine that for readers of these lectures, 3 and 4 are the only live options, and I may be the only one to take 4 seriously. No matter. On either 3 or 4, Nature must be an artful modeler . . . because there is no book to go by. Both give up on the book in denying type-type reduction,[16] which is the one view that assumes there are proper principles to describe the relations of features across levels.

1. i c Millikan's experiment: How to think of Stokes's principle

Before leaving physics, let's return to the oil drop experiment for illustration. Millikan used Stokes's principle to calculate F_{drag}. In the decades after publishing his results, he and others, in particular Paul Epstein, developed a theoretical underpinning for the version of Stokes's formula Millikan used. Their efforts show how a single principle—Stokes's[17]—gets turned into a

---

[16] As is often noted, this does not follow from multiple-realizability by itself. If the supervenience base for a given feature is finite, type-type reductions can be obtained by disjunction over the base options. Or if the supervenience base-states all have something in common not shared with other states, then that can be ascribed at the base level, a common feature that can serve for type-type reduction.

[17] Or better, as I shall explain in note 26, 'near-propositions'.

variety of different context-dependent propositions.[18] Although I think talk of a hierarchy of levels is a mistake, I will use the labels 'macro' and 'micro' here to make vivid how much crossing of 'levels' is going on.

Stokes's principle calculates the drag force on a sphere in a fluid thus:

$$\text{Equation 1.1: } \mathbf{F}_{\text{drag}} = 6\pi\alpha\mu v.$$

Here α is the radius of the sphere, μ the viscosity of the fluid, and v the velocity of the sphere—all macro quantities.

I propose we view Stokes's principle as a building block that we use, sometimes intact and sometimes with adjustments, to construct the detailed models we use to predict and manage the world, much like Thomas Kuhn's 'law schema'.[19] Suppose we want to turn Equation 1.1 into a well-formed proposition. From standard accounts of Stokes's principle we already know we must be careful with the conditions of application, which include:

- For the spheres
  - Small (macro)
  - Smooth-surfaced (macro)
  - Rigid (macro)
  - No other particles in vicinity (macro)
- For the fluid
  - Homogeneous (macro)
  - Incompressible (macro)
  - Non-turbulent (macro)
  - Constituent particles do not interfere with each other (micro)

We might then try something like this:

Equation 1.1': (x) [If x is a small, smooth-surfaced, rigid, spherical body of radius α and velocity v, distant from other macroscopic bodies, and is settling in a non-turbulent, homogeneous, incompressible fluid of viscosity μ whose constituent particles do not interfere with each other, then $\mathbf{F}_{\text{drag}}(x) = 6\pi\alpha\mu v$.][20]

---

[18] Always with the NE rider.

[19] See the "Postscript" to the *Structure of Scientific Revolutions*, 182–89; "Logic of Discovery or Psychology of Research?," 18–19; and "Reflections on My Critics" in Lakatos and Musgrave 1972.

[20] This looks to me to have just the form recommended by Friend 2016.

We would certainly not, though, wish to eliminate the non-propositionalized equation 1.1 and make do only with 1.1' and its consequences. Why? Because 1.1 is the starting place from which a vast number of other context-specific formulae are built.

Millikan's modeling is a case in point. Note that Stokes's formula is for a fluid—a continuous medium.[21] Air is not continuous, and this can make a significant difference when the radius of the sphere is small compared with the mean free path length, l, of the molecules in the medium: the medium offers less resistance than formula 1.1 provides. To take into account the particulate nature of air, Millikan added a correction factor to 1.1:

$$\text{Equation 1.2: } F_{drag} = 6\pi a \mu v / (1 + Al/a).$$

Here A is, in Millikan's own words, "an undetermined constant."[22]

Millikan and Epstein both attempted a "careful theoretical examination" of Millikan's correction, deriving formulae for F_{drag} from the assumption that it is entirely due to 'molecules' of 'air' impinging on and leaving the surface of the sphere.[23] Here is a list of additional conditions supposed in their treatments beyond those already mentioned:

- For the spheres
  - Non-rotating (macro)
  - May be conducting or non-conducting (macro)
- For the molecules
  - Molecules impinging on the sphere: they have a Maxwell distribution for their velocities (micro and macro, since the Maxwell distribution is a function of the temperature of the gas)
  - Molecules leaving the sphere do so in a mix of these ways
    - Uniform evaporation
    - Specular reflection

---

[21] Note also that it may be that there aren't any continuous media, which already makes trouble for taking formulae to be making true claims about the world.

[22] He adds: "It is to be particularly emphasized that the term in the brackets was expressly set up merely as a first order correction term in l/a and involved no theoretical assumptions of any sort; further that the constant A was empirically determined . . ." We should note too that Millikan attributed the changes in the value for the charge of the electron from the experiments in his 1911 paper to those in his 1913 paper in part to improvements in his empirical estimate of the correction factor for Stokes's law.

[23] See for example, Epstein 1924. I put 'molecules' and 'air' in scare quotes because these molecules have no internal structure and are of no particular kind; they are just tiny moving, non-interfering objects.

- Diffuse reflection, no change in Maxwell velocity distribution
- Diffuse reflection with change in velocity distribution, which behaves differently depending on whether the sphere is conducting or non-conducting
  - Non-conducting sphere where the velocity distribution = Maxwell distribution for the effective temperature of the surface they are reflected from
  - Conducting sphere where the velocity distribution = Maxwell distribution for the effective temperature of the surface they are reflected from.

There are a number of things to note about this before we leave Millikan.

(1) I count 15 conditions,[24] each associated with a different development of Stokes's principle. And each has alternatives that can occur together in a large variety of different combinations: What if the sphere is large and smooth . . . ? Large and not smooth . . . ? Not smooth in which ways? What if a small smooth sphere is in a turbulent medium . . . ? Etc. Also these are features just taken from the discussion of the oil drop experiment and that, only up to 1925. Physics and engineering continue to produce developments of Stokes's principle today, especially in aeronautics, astrophysics, plasma physics, and the study of aerosols and pollutants.

(2) Each of these many formulae can be recast as a proper, highly-conditioned, proposition—so long as my nothing-else rider (NE) is included among the conditions.

(3) These are probably true; they can be counted in the body of our knowledge-that. What cannot be situated there is any true proposition with genuine content that covers them all. They are not *derived from* some proposition associated with Stokes's principle; they are *built using* it.[25]

(4) Once the conditions are added in, we see that features from different 'levels' act together.

---

[24] Spheres: Small, smooth, non-rotating, conducting or non-conducting, rigid, no others nearby = 6; Fluid: non-turbulent, incompressible, non-interfering constituents, Maxwell distribution on impinging molecules, ratios and descriptions for the 4 distinct ways molecules may leave, kind of velocity distribution for diffusely reflected molecules = 9.

[25] In the best of pure theory cases, the building is principled. For instance, in arriving at the formula for large spheres in a gas of uniform temperature, which because of their size influence the motion of the gas molecules, Epstein uses Boltzmann's H theorem to calculate the distribution of velocities. But these latter principles, like Stokes's itself, don't function in this process as proper propositions from which the requisite consequences can be deduced.

(5) We have still not arrived at claims about specific real-world systems. These will always have an indefinite number of other features that do not figure in the conditions considered so far, and in some cases these will be relevant to the outcome, violating the NE rider. Yet we may well be able to build a formula for F_{drag} in these cases starting from Stokes's principle.[26]

1. ii Where Rules for Arrangements Give Out

Let's now look at a case far from physics, which is where the bulk of our modeling takes place, an example from the Nature Conservancy. They've got to get it right about what will happen when they act; and they use a lot of science to help them. They do not do it by the book, and I've no idea what the book would be like that they could do it by. Yet they often do it very well. I want to focus on the lack of rules to guide them on what happens when features, even well understood features, act together in new arrangements. The Nature Conservancy deals with real ecologies, which have lots of intimately interacting parts whose exact arrangement matters. There are many 'rules of thumb', practiced experience, and a lot of 'common sense' to help, but there are no proper principles in the offing. This is a paradigm of artful modeling.

Their models generally look like Figure 1.4, which is for a marine reserve.

Here I'll consider a verbal version of a model, this one for the attempt to save the native Santa Cruz Island foxes, which were dying out. The proposal was to establish protected breeding sites for the foxes. Will this lead to a viable fox population?[27]

The Nature Conservancy began with a causal model of why the foxes were disappearing. They were being eaten by golden eagles, who came attracted by feral pigs and by wild turkeys. The golden eagles were in overabundance because DDT in the water had killed off the bald eagles who prey on the golden eagles.

This causal model spawned the blueprint for intervention. If the model for the fox disappearance is correct, establishing protected breeding sites can only lead to more foxes if the golden eagles are reduced. So simultaneously with setting up the breeding sites, the plan was to get rid of the golden eagles. But this couldn't be done by lethal take permits due to predicted political

---

[26] Or, starting from some formulae already developed for some subset of the relevant features. It is for this reason that I used the term 'near-propositions' in note 17. To turn them into proper propositions that are plausibly true, we need the NE rider, which them makes them far less applicable. So it is best to leave them in their non-propositionalized form.

[27] To read more see https://www.ns.gov/chis/learn/nature/fox-decline.htm.

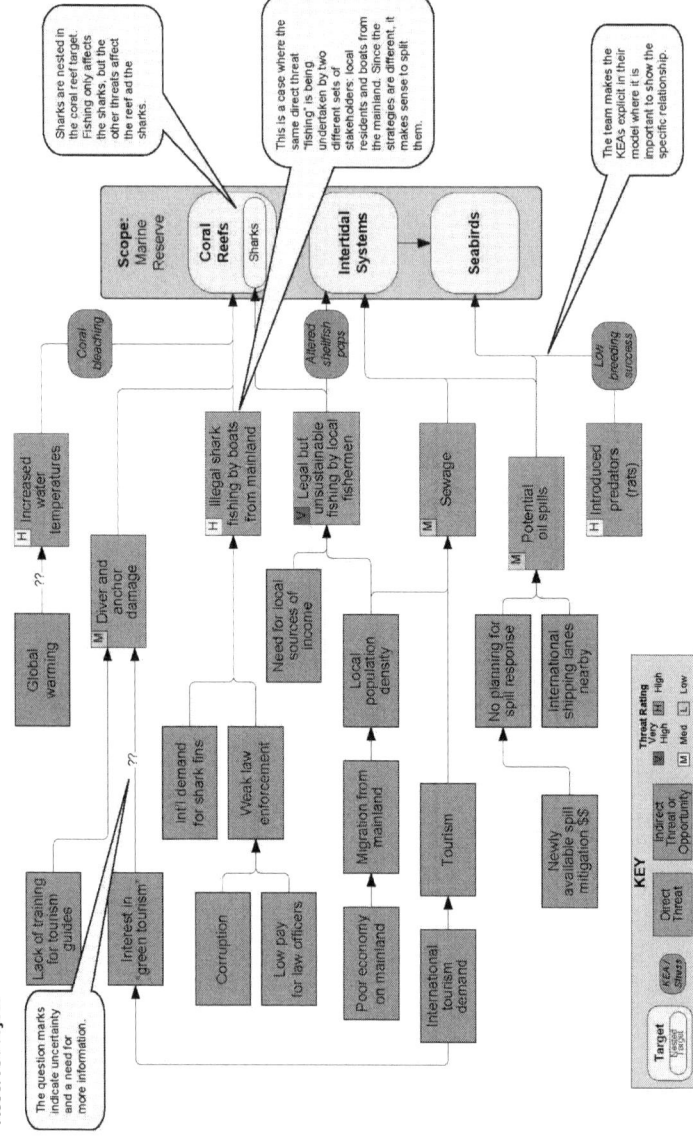

Figure 1.4 Nature Conservancy Model for a Marine Reserve. Reprinted with permission from: TNC, 2007. *Conservation Action Planning Handbook: Developing Strategies, Taking Action and Measuring Success at Any Scale.* The Nature Conservancy, Arlington, VA.

fallout.[28] So it was to be done by tranquilizers, fishnets, and helicopter-fired net guns. At the same time as breeding foxes in captivity and removing some golden eagles, it would also be necessary to:

- Reintroduce bald eagles
- Eliminate the wild turkeys
- Eliminate thousands of feral pigs.

This meant bringing in a team of sharp shooters from New Zealand.

- These may be stopped by animal rights suits.

So

- Be sure the Conservancy can win these suits (there were five in all);

And

- Be sure the Conservancy is right to do so.

The interventions undertaken, following this predictive causal model, proved successful. The survival rate on the baby foxes is 90 percent and there are now over 700 foxes on the island.

This is a paradigm of artful modeling, done well. But it is done without appeal to general rules for calculating what happens when these different causes act together as they will, given the arrangements on Santa Cruz Island. How could there be such rules? *There are too many possible arrangements of too many possible causes, mixed across levels and domains.*[29] Know-how is all that's left to get the job done.

1. iii In Review

Successful predictions are not derived from general principles but constructed by artful modeling. The first argument for this, which I do not

---

[28] Predicted how? From knowledge of the local anti-hunting sympathies, the laws about lethal take permits, the psychology, level of organization, and economic resources of those opposed to killing the golden eagles, research that elsewhere golden eagles are endangered, and more.

[29] And there's no evidence that all the possible arrangements of all the possible causes of all the possible kinds can be cast into classes that fall under meta-rules: 'For arrangements of type A, use rule of composition α; of type B, use β; etc.'

review here, is that this is what the empirical evidence shows, from studies across the history, sociology, and philosophy of science. It is difficult to find a single example of a real-world prediction about concrete, embodied systems that is done by the book.

Second, this follows from a far stronger claim: This is as it must be, for there is no book to go by. There couldn't be. There are too many features interacting in too many ways, in too many possible arrangements, and mixed across levels and domains, for outcomes to follow the dictates of general principles. There is no choice but local know-how.

2. Nature, the Artful Modeler

If we are artful modelers, as I claim we must be, our scientific understanding of the world does not reside in knowledge-that but in knowledge-how. What does it mean for know-how of the kind we display to be *knowledge*-how? To explore this question, let us think about scientific realism—which will need to be reconceptualized if there is no book to go by.

2. i Scientific Realism Reconfigured

Know-how is sometimes associated with instrumentalism. I am not defending instrumentalism. First, for the reason I am about to explore. Instrumentalism is traditionally a form of anti-realism. But nothing in my argument blocks us having genuine knowledge. Second, I do not deny that there may be real entities referred to by theoretical common names, like *electron, DNA,* or *democratic peace,* and real quantities and qualities referred to by theoretical variables and concepts, like *potential difference, spin, psychological priming, utility.* I have long argued that, by all ordinary standards of good evidence, we have good evidence that some of these concepts refer and some do not. Third, I also take it that some principles can be expressed as propositions and are so well supported that we should count them true, in the ordinary sense in which other matters are true. For instance, 'All electrons have the same charge, of 1.6×10^{-19} Coulombs' or 'Most neurons have multiple dendrites'.[30]

---

[30] I also take it that a number of plausibly true situation-specific propositions employing 'theoretical' concepts will be formulable from the models we use to generate predictions. But the issue here is not about local scientific claims that are supported by a model but rather about the scientific knowledge used to generate the model.

What I have struggled with, ever since my first book, *How the Laws of Physics Lie*, is that a great many of our cherished and most useful scientific principles, cannot be well-formulated. As I have been arguing here, I see no way to formulate them so that:

1. They say something that could be true or false—they are well formed enough to express a proposition.
2. What they say could be in the ballpark of true.
3. They have a serious body of empirical support. This means they must meet at least two demands:
    a) They need to cover (most of) the well-supported context-dependent propositions which we formulate using them. We have seen in Part 1 that this makes a big problem.
    b) They must not generalize far beyond the domains in which they have passed severe tests.
4. They can do the work we put them to in prediction and design.
5. They have genuine content. This is what Popper called for in his demand that scientific claims be falsifiable. Adler and Freud could explain anything because there were too few rules connecting their theoretical concepts with the world. We can do the same in any theory. There's no problem rendering '**F** = m**a**' as a universal well-formed formula. For instance, L = (x)[**F**(x) = m(x)**a**(x)], where the domain of quantification is massive objects. But this claim only has genuine content so long as **F**(x) is assigned by rule rather than, say, by back calculation from m(x) and **a**(x). But this, I claim, is what is generally done in defence of the universal claim.[31]

I have floated what I think is the only plausible proposal for how to turn principles into propositions that respects requirement 3b, viz.:

- Take your best effort at rendering your scientific principle in a form that expresses a proposition, maybe for instance L above for Newton's law:

$$L = (x)[\mathbf{F}(x) = m(x)\mathbf{a}(x)]$$

- Then offer λ, which is essentially L with the 'nothing else' rider attached as the properly propositionalized law claim:

---

[31] Cartwright 1999.

> λ: So long as nothing operates to affect the consequence described in L except things that can be represented with the concepts in the antecedent of L, then L.

Unfortunately there are big problems for λ. Perhaps we can allow that λ satisfies conditions 1, 2, and 3. But the condition at the start is seldom satisfied, so λ can do little, thus violating condition 4.

So: I do not think these requirements can be satisfied at once. Nor do our scientific successes speak for a need for this. As I have urged, our successful models are not secured by rule-governed derivation from empirically well-supported claims. To build the Oxford knee, measure the charge of an electron, evacuate Fort McMurray, or save the Santa Cruz Island foxes, we use our accumulated scientific and practical knowledge. We may use the concepts, the ideas, the exact functional form of our laws; but we use them as 'symbolic representations'. For predicting and manipulating the world around us, we rely on know-how.

What then of scientific realism? Laying aside the existence of theoretical entities, the debates in scientific realism have to do with the truth of scientific principles.[32] If my arguments are correct, these debates are mis-focused.

Imagine, first, that you are a scientific skeptic. Perhaps because our concepts are socially constructed, or perhaps because post-lapsarians will never get it right in this life (nor deserve to), or because we are trapped, like brains in a vat, in a merely phenomenal world. Or conversely, suppose you are a believer: It would be a miracle indeed if our precise predictions are borne out again and again and our science-based technology works if we are not getting it right. In either case, your eye should not be on principles but on practice, not on truth but on know-how. The question should not be:

> Are our scientific principles (or selected aspects of them) true (true enough, approaching the truth . . .)?

But rather

> Is our know-how *know*-how; do our successful practices constitute genuine knowledge?

---

[32] Or aspects of them like their structure, which is central to structural realism. The structure in our most credible models of embodied systems may mimic the structure of relations in the world. But the same problems arise for getting these structures to be ones properly prescribed by theory.

Hasok Chang argues that it is. What he calls "knowledge-as-ability" is *knowledge*, he argues, on the grounds of the pragmatist coherence of our system of epistemic activities, where pragmatist coherence is the "harmonious fitting-together of actions that leads to the successful achievement of one's aims."[33] I want to add to this. Our know-how can be genuine knowledge not only on the grounds of the coherence of our activities and the successes of our practices but because of a fit with the world:

> Our practices are successful because we do it the way Nature does;
> we use Nature's resources to recoup Nature's happenings.

By 'doing it the way Nature does' I mean that the best way to recoup the happenings in the world is the way we do it, by artful modeling. There is no better system, unbeknownst to us, that Nature is following, no hidden scheme that organizes and predicts happening better. To assess this claim, let us consider what Nature's happenings are like.

2. ii *The Scientific Image*

The *scientific image* is our account of what the world is like taken from the perspective of contemporary science.[34] It depicts what we think Nature's happenings are like. How should we construct this image?

I urge firm empiricism: Short steps from what we see to what we claim there is, not high flights of fancy or great leaps of faith. On this empiricist strategy, we should construct our image of the world that the sciences study from how our sciences study it when they are most successful at getting it right.[35] This makes life hard for laws of nature as traditionally conceived. Where is our argument that there is any such thing in reality when we don't find proper law claims in our sciences?

---

[33] Chang 2017, 113. He is currently developing this idea in detail for his prospective book, *Realism for Realistic People: A New Pragmatist Philosophy of Science*.

[34] By 'science' I intend the German sense, *Wissenschaft*, 'The systematic pursuit of knowledge, learning, and scholarship.' (Oxford Living Dictionaries 2018)

[35] I am here buying into Jean Roberts's 'Science-Says-So Thesis' that we can be justified in believing that the laws of nature govern the universe without appealing to any extra-scientific source of epistemic justification, at least read as claiming that science is the only source of epistemic justification admissible. I agree that this source is all that is admissible and that it is admissible—it simply doesn't support the conclusion that laws of nature govern (or describe) the universe (Roberts 2008, 26).

Robin Hendry describes this form of empiricism as supposing "a commitment to explanatory realism (i.e. we can infer things about nature from explanations)." But, he adds—and this is what is at the heart of the commitment to empiricism—"explanatory realism should be limited to those parts of a theory that do important scientific work." Hendry offers our use of 'approximate methods' as illustration, voicing a strong opposition to what he describes as

> the 'proxy view' . . . in which . . . [approximate methods] stand in for exact methods which 'in principle' can do the same explanatory work. The problem is that that assumption is only very rarely justified mathematically, and there are often principled/foundational difficulties in providing one. . . . Instead one should take the approximate methods seriously, seeing them as reflecting real (kinds of) physical conditions. . . .
> [T]o be able to use a general physical theory to describe a kind of phenomenon (e.g. planetary motion), one needs to find the right approximate starting point . . . , e.g. breaking the Newtonian solar system down into a series of perturbed two-body problems, allowing heuristic advances like helping oneself to the conic sections. . . . That's what is actually doing the explanatory work, not . . . a mathematical function representing the dynamical state of the solar system as a whole. . . . The maths doesn't support the existence of such an n-body function, and it plays no role in the ongoing scientific work. It's the conic sections that are important.[36]

---

[36] Hendry 2017. Hendry also offers a detailed case from his own work: "An example I have been working on with Robert Schoonmaker is how, in general, one can account for molecular structure within quantum mechanics. Approximate methods such as the adiabatic approximation correspond to situations in which various important symmetries of molecular Hamiltonians are suppressed. For instance, interactions among a group of nuclei are mediated by their joint interaction with a local field of electron density, which among other things suppresses particle permutation symmetries (effectively, it doesn't matter from an energetic point of view if you treat them classically as the probability of any two identical nuclei swapping places is low enough). This allows the internuclear structure to be thought of as inhabiting a potential energy surface, which is a great heuristic advance, but can only be applied within the bounds of applicability of the adiabatic approximation.

The more usual explanation for molecular structure is that one solves the Schrodinger equation for a molecule (using approximations which could in principle be discarded), yielding the molecular states. The problem is that the approximations CANNOT be discarded, and the Schrodinger equation applies to far too many kinds of state for anything useful to be derivable from it alone. The specific assumptions (built into the approximate methods) MUST, from a mathematical point of view, be doing ineliminable explanatory work. Another familiar example would be the renormalisation group."

The proxy story has it that Nature creates the orbits in accord with an n-body function. It supposes that the orbits are as they must be if some proposition with that n-body function at its core is to be true. Suppose, as I've been arguing, that no such proposition is formulable.[37] What then are the orbits like? Following the empiricist methodology I advocate, they are as we calculate them to be, using the formulae we use—"It's the conic sections that are important." They are in accord with our model. This is an 'artful model', done with know-how, not 'by the book'. 'Nature does it the way we do it' implies that the orbits that obtain are the ones we predict.

Our modeling may be artful but getting the right answer is no miracle. It rests on detailed expertise and training and a vast concerted community effort. Often, if pressed, we can articulate reasons why it should be done this way rather than that on this occasion, but not reasons that can be turned into general principles. We see analogies among situations, similarities and differences; we learn that these similarities and differences are likely to matter in this kind of situation and not that, though we cannot give a description of 'this kind' and 'that kind' that turns this into a general truth. We rely on not only on complex mathematical formulae, like those characteristic in physics theory, but also on a vast array of context-specific 'rough-and-ready principles' throughout our scientific, technological, and engineering modeling, like

- Bring up a child in the way he shall go, and when he is grown he shall not depart from it
- Rising levels of inflation cause lowering levels of unemployment
- The planets circulate the sun in elliptical orbits.

Sometimes these begin with the vague quantifier 'generally', which may make them sound like proper propositions that can figure in deductions. If John Norton is to be believed—as I think he should be—these rough-and-ready principles are at the heart of much of our inductive inference. They guide us in regarding one situation as similar to another with respect to transferring effects from one to the other. Norton asks why Marie Curie could assume

---

[37] Perhaps, 'Whenever n massive objects interact gravitationally and all other interactions, either among themselves or with other objects, add a vector δ to their accelerations, then the vector of their accelerations is given by $X + \delta$', where X is the n-body function. But a proposition of this form is always true until we put sufficient constraints on what δ can be. And doing that in accord with a properly propositionalized principle faces the same problems.

that some of the features of the radium chloride she studied in her lab would hold in other samples, but other features were not expected to. He answers

> [W]hy [should] the schema . . . be limited precisely to the few properties of radium chloride that Curie so confidently generalized[?] The justification . . . lies in the researches of chemists in the nineteenth century . . . [in] "Haüy's Principle": . . . *Generally*, each crystalline substance has a single characteristic crystallographic form. . . . That means that once one has found the characteristic crystallographic form of some sample of a substance, *generally* one knows it for all samples.[38]

Note the repeated use of 'generally'. It is clever, informed, experienced, context-specific use of this principle in the hands of someone like Marie Curie that gets the right answers.

Returning to the central discussion of the scientific image, let us focus for a moment on the Mill-Ramsey-Lewis view of scientific laws (MRL): The correct set of laws is the smallest set of general claims from which follow the largest number of facts. For many, the 'facts' are about Humean features. I shall not assume that; let the facts be what they may. The problem with MRL is that it supposes a scientific image we are not entitled to. We do not marshal the facts under general law claims; and the facts we predict are not in accord with any such claims. Still, we can exploit the basic idea of MRL to help describe the world that science studies.

The point of laws for MRL is to recoup the facts: to get hold of as many facts as possible in the most efficient way possible. If I am correct, we do not do this by derivation from general propositions; we do it by artful modelling. That's the way we recoup the facts. Empiricist methodology instructs us to construct the scientific image of the world closely from how we succeed in predicting and manipulating it. So we had best suppose that this is the way the world is. The facts are not totally disorderly, else no success in prediction or manipulation would be possible. But they cannot be summed up in any set of scientific-law-like propositions.

2. iii Speaking of Realism: Nature? Modeling? Really?

No, not 'really'. 'Nature the artful modeler' is a metaphor. Some may think it an unfortunate metaphor, more obfuscating than illuminating. I disagree.

---
[38] Norton 2014, 10 (my emphasis).

It is more apt than 'Nature the enforcer of laws', laws writ we know not where; and that in turn, because enforcement generally has patchy results, is more apt to the world as we actually find it than are laws, writ we know not where, that are directly—without an enforcing mediator—responsible for what happens, or that, Mill-Ramsey-Lewis style, happenings conform to despite their lack of all authority. 'Nature the artful modeler' is more apt than these because it has no truck with laws. Our success at modeling the world with knowledge from science and engineering gives us little evidence for these laws—indeed, it seems to give us evidence to the contrary; and I can find no good reason for them other than faith.

To maintain that Nature is an artful modeler is to take seriously that the way we capture the happenings in the world when we do it successfully is probably the very best way there is, since we have no evidence that there is any other way to do the job. There is no way to get more—no way for more predictability nor for more reliability, even if we were released from our human limitations. The happenings in Nature do not lend themselves to more systematic summary.

So, I claim that Nature is an artful modeler to keep the empiricist dictate that I urged at the start of section 2ii: to read what the patterns of happenings are from our best methods for capturing those happenings; and to refrain from leaps of faith that there's some way, quite different from what we do, to do it better. There is no fuller, neater, more orderly scheme to the events in Nature, no scheme that perhaps Adam could see before the fall, or maybe Leibniz's demon, or the fabulous creature who can take a view from nowhere.

In Sum

We should take our scientific successes as our guide, as empiricism dictates. In which case, we should conclude that most likely there is no more efficient way to recoup the facts than the way we do it. What happens in the world can be recouped by artful modeling because that is what the world is like. Nature herself—like us—is an artful modeler.

2

Nature's Raw Materials

Powers, arrangements, and causes. She manages actual possibilities, obeys the Barcan formula, and does not sit down with counterfactuals.

INTRODUCTION

This lecture begins in Section 1 with some of the basic resources we—and Nature—call upon in predicting what will come to pass: powers and their exercise.[39] Powers are popular in metaphysics nowadays, often in the hunt for a monistic ontology, as in pan-dispositionalism. My arguments are rooted differently. I back powers because they help make sense of the widespread success of some of our favorite scientific methods. This is in accord with the empiricist dictum I urged in Lecture 1: Construct our scientific image of the world from our scientific practices that prove successful in interacting with it. Here I will look at three specific kinds of practice:

- The analytic method
- Our treatments of probabilistic causes
- Post hoc evaluation of policy effectiveness.

---

[39] My own term for causal powers has long been 'capacities', to avoid identification with any notion of powers that assumes they can be given a conditional analysis as it seemed to me that Harré and Madden 1975 had supposed. I also used the term 'nomological machines' for what are now popularly discussed, especially in philosophy of biology, under the heading 'mechanisms'. Here I talk about *arrangements* of powers. A nomological machine is an arrangement of powers that, if set working repeatedly, would give rise to the kinds of patterns of happenings that 'laws of nature' are typically thought to describe. If we suppose that the powers that are at work in an arrangement and the rules of combination that apply to them are *reliable* in the senses that I shall explain, then that arrangement will be a nomological machine, supposing that we allow that 'laws of nature' need not be 'deterministic' but instead might designate some restricted set of outcomes rather than one unique outcome.

The discussion of the analytic method in Section 1 will be the longest. It is where I develop the kind of powers ontology—called a 'Trias' ontology—that I think we need. It is also where a good while ago I got off on the wrong foot about powers and the contributions we use to label them. My original hope was to use powers and contributions to render the principles deployed in the analytic method true. This is a mistake. As with the scientific principles I discussed in Lecture 1, these are formulae, not propositions. Nor do we need them to be propositions for the uses to which we put them. We need powers to make sense of the successes of the analytic method but not to turn our formulae into true claims.

Section 2 rejects the almost universally accepted connection between powers and conditionals. Powers don't need conditionals to speak for them, and these putative conditionals can no more be rendered as true propositions than the scientific principles I discussed in Lecture 1.

Section 3 looks at possibility and contingency, at how Nature operates with these, and in particular at how contingent her outcomes are. The future it seems is very often not very settled. Meccano aficionados and car mechanics refer to this as 'the cussedness of machines'. You build it by the book, but there is always more going on than even your concepts, let alone your principles, can cover. As I argued in Lecture 1, there are indefinitely many features and indefinitely many conceivable arrangements of them, too many for laws to cover. Nature is on her own here. She must plump, as do we when we make a reasonable bet on an outcome. This leaves us with a world much as we experience it: with endless possibilities but where it is difficult to secure the ones we'd like, even with heroic efforts.

1. Powers and Their Role in Scientific Practice

1. i Powers and the Analytic Method

1. i a The analytic method

We use the analytic method to construct reliable models across a wide range of subject matters and contexts. In keeping with my thesis that Nature does it the way we do, I hypothesize that Nature too makes wide use of the analytic method. Powers are the basic resources for doing so. To explain this, I need to go over some old ground.

I began my career with the book *How the Laws of Physics Lie*. One of the sources of the lies I described is the analytic method. There seems to be no way to formulate the base principles—those that describe the 'canonical' behaviors of individual features—as laws in any way that satisfies the five requirements for laws from Lecture 1, in particular, there seems to be no way to render them as both true and able to do the jobs of explanation and prediction that we expect of them. At least there seems to be no way to do so sticking within an ontology 'without modalities' or that admits only 'Humean' features.[40]

Let us begin with the paradigm of the analytic method since at least J. S. Mill: mechanics and its force functions. For illustration, consider a propositionalized version of the theory presupposed in Figure 1.1 from Lecture 1 describing Millikan's oil drop experiment.

There are three kinds of principles in my caricature Millikan theory (CMT): Principles that describe what the features in the analytic base (gravity, charge, drag) 'contribute to' the force[41] on the oil drop, (LoG, LoC, SL), a principle (sometimes called a 'law of composition') that says what force occurs when they act together (LoC), and a principle that says what happens to the acceleration of the oil drops (NLM):

CMT:

LoG (Law of Gravity): (x) [x is a mass M a distance $\mathbf{r}$ from mass m → x contributes $F_G = GMm/\mathbf{r}^2$ to the force on m]

CL (Coulomb's Law): (x) [x is a charge q_2 a distance $\mathbf{r}$ from charge q_1 → x contributes $F_e = \varepsilon q_1 q_2 /\mathbf{r}^2$ to the force on q_1]

SL (Stokes's Law): (x) [x is ordinary air → x contributes a drag $F_{drag} = 6\pi a\mu v/(1 + Al/a)$ to the force on any small, smooth-surfaced, rigid, isolated sphere falling through it]

LoC (Law of Composition): The force on an object = vector sum (⊕) of all the contributions it is subject to.

NLM (Newton's Law of Motion): An object of mass m subject to force $\mathbf{F}$ has an acceleration, $\mathbf{a} = \mathbf{F}/m$.

---

[40] I know no way to characterize this special de-modalized ontology that cuts it the way I think advocates of de-modalization want. But I propose we go with Barry Loewer's account (1996) of what David Lewis meant by a 'Humean' feature in order to move forward: "Call a property 'Humean' if its instantiation requires no more than a spatio-temporal point and its instantiation at that point has no metaphysical implications concerning the instantiations of fundamental properties elsewhere and elsewhen. Lewis's examples of Humean properties are the values of electromagnetic and gravitational fields and the presence/absence of a material particle at a point" (Loewer 1996, 102).

[41] Note that I talk here of 'the force' rather than 'the total force' because, on the powers ontology I lay out here, what is called the 'total' force is the only force there is. What appears on the right-hand side in LoG and CL are, I shall argue, just formulae associated with the power of gravity and the Coulomb power that we often know how to use to calculate the force a body will experience.

I remind you that both Newton's law and Stokes's must be read with the nothing-else rider (NE) attached to the antecedents if they are to have any chance of being true, which is philosophy of science's cheap way to handle finks, antidotes, masks, defeaters, interferences, and the like. Right now, it is the consequents that are at issue. What we see there are not proper Humean quantities; component forces should not appear in a Humean ontology. Why?

Following Albert Einstein and Leopold Infeld: "[T]he action of an external force changes the velocity [of an object on which it is exerted].... Such a force either increases or decreases the velocity according to whether it acts in the direction of motion or in the opposite direction."[42] So, forces cause motions. If there is nothing but forces to take into account in the determination of a motion,[43] they do so according to the formula $\mathbf{F} = m\mathbf{a}$. If we allow that the component forces and the total force are all really present forces, we get contradictory motions. Nor should we think of the 'component' forces as parts, like the left-hand side and the right-hand side of a block of fused quartz.[44] Vector addition is not addition; it is not mereology; it is not the glomming together of parts. If two of us each lays $5 on the table, there will ipso facto be $10 on the table. If the sun lays a gravitational force of 3.6×10^{22} Newtons on the earth, and the moon lays a force of 1.98×10^{20} Newtons on it, those two piled together do not ipso facto constitute the total force of the sun and moon on the earth. So, the principles in the analytic base are not made true by the mere obtaining of the total force.

How then should we read these base principles? My next major work, in 1989, was *Nature's Capacities and Their Measurement*. The capacities I introduced and defended there[45] are a version of what are now commonly called 'causal powers'. One of the arguments I used in their defense is that they allow us to render as true the principles in the analytic base. I now see that this is a mistake. But let's get there by steps.

---

[42] Einstein and Infeld 1938, 10.

[43] I add this caveat because of requirement 5 from Lecture 1 for acceptable propositionalization of a law claim. 'Force' is a proper theoretical term with rules—bridge principles—for what forms it can take under what conditions. In many specific cases there are obvious causes of motion that do not appear to fall under these rules. There may of course be hidden facts about these causal factors that bring them under the rules, but, I argue (see for example Cartwright 1999), our successes in using Newtonian physics do not provide evidence for this.

[44] For why fused quartz is an especially good example here, see Lecture 3, section 6.

[45] By arguing, for instance, that capacities can be just as measurable as the quantities usually labeled 'Humean'.

1. i b A Trias powers ontology

'Contributions' and the exercise of powers
On the powers ontology I urge, the principles in the analytic base simultaneously pinpoint a power—they tell us what power it is—and provide an independently identifiable condition for its occurrence. They tell us what the power is by labeling it with a formula that we—and Nature—use to help calculate what happens to an associated kind of outcome when that power acts. For example, the 'law' of gravity is not to be rendered as a proposition, as with LoG. Rather, it makes more sense of our practice to see this as a principle that tells us that the power dubbed 'the power of gravity' can influence the force on a body of mass m located **r** away. This principle attaches a label to this power —$GMm/\mathbf{r}^2$—that we know how to deploy in calculating what happens when that power influences an outcome of the kind associated with it—the force a distant body experiences. It also tells us that that power will obtain in any body that has mass M.[46]

Powers don't just obtain. They don't always just sit there, inertly. Sometimes they act—they exercise—and in exercising they influence outcomes of the kind they are associated with, they help make them happen. The exercising is essential. If each of the powers did not influence the outcome when they act in consort, we wouldn't see the effects we do. So, there is a distinction between the obtaining of a power and its acting to influence (helping to fix) an outcome, as well as between its acing to influence an outcome and the obtaining of that outcome. There are thus three components in this kind of powers ontology: the obtaining of a power, the exercising of a power, and the obtaining of an outcome. I follow Florian Fischer in calling powers like his and mine 'Trias' powers to mark this three-fold ontology.[47]

---

[46] Note that there is nothing implied here about what category these independently identifiable features (like mass) fall into—sui generis properties, collections of powers, or whatever. It is worth underlining though that the same independently identifiable feature, like mass or charge, may be/be associated with/bring with it a variety of different powers.

[47] My view here is Aristotelian, at least as Anna Marmodoro would have it. She explains that for Aristotle what she (and some others) calls the *manifestation* of the power "is the activation of the power, either as it is exercising its influence on the passive power or as the passive power is suffering that influence. For example, if a mango has the power to ripen in the heat, the ripening is the actualisation of active and passive powers at play. The ripe state of the mango that comes about is the 'aftermath' of the activation of the powers, not their manifestation. The powers are manifested in their activity with each other, not in the state that results from their activation" (2018). I differ, however, in not distinguishing active and passive powers. Though I have nothing against passive powers, these don't play a part in the argument from the successes of the analytic method to a powers ontology, so

It is the capacity to influence outcomes that earns a Trias power its right to the label 'power', given the simple conceptual connection between being powerful and being able to affect the course of events. Hume took this middle item—the exercising—to be essential to the concept of a power. He thought that, if there are powers, there should be a distinction between the obtaining of a power and its exercise and between its exercise and the obtaining of the effect. Since he couldn't find any such distinctions in his experience, he denied powers a place among his ideas of the external world.

I have tried to be careful here to use the terms 'influencing' and 'exercising'. But I have not always done so. I used to speak of powers and *the contributions they make*. This was misleading. 'Contribution' was introduced as a technical term. It was not meant to name something of the same type as the actually occurring effect, and it would be a mistake to try to see it as part of the effect in any reasonable sense of 'part'. I already noted that vector addition is not addition. It might be possible to be more forgiving on this if addition or vector addition were the universal rules for calculating what happens when different powers act together (so-called 'rules of combination'). But they are far from it. I have argued this in the past (most notably in *The Dappled World*) but to reinforce it I have more recently done further work on rules of combination.

Here for instance is just one of a great many equations from economics I could cite, this from a paper by Nobel-prize-winning labor market expert Christopher Pissarides.[48] Pissarides tells us about the value V of a vacancy and J of an occupied job:

The Bellman equations giving their values are,

$$rV = -\kappa A + q(J - V) + \dot{V}$$
$$rJ = A - w - \lambda J + \dot{J}$$

where A is the product per worker; κA, the cost of holding a vacancy; q, the transition rate of a typical vacancy; and r, a discount factor.

I don't take a stand on them. Powers act together in arrangements to produce outcomes (where I stay neutral about the metaphysical status of an outcome); they act *together* but not on each other. I also avoid the term *manifestation* since it is used both for this third element, which John Pemberton and I now call the *exercising* of the power, and also for the outcome of their joint action (Cartwright and Pemberton 2013).

[48] Pissarides 2007.

He also tells us:

> The wage rate is assumed to be a weighted average of the unemployed worker's income and the output per person:
>
> $w = (1 - \beta_0)b + \beta_0 A, \quad \beta_0 \in (0, 1)$[49]

where *b* is the income of an unemployed worker.

In this case no one would think that the value of a vacancy has three distinct pieces, each there in the same way that the value of the vacancy is, nor that there are two proper pieces of wage rate that occur along with the actual wage rate.

Look to boxes 2.1 to 2.6 for further examples. These illustrate what happens across a number of subjects when powers contribute together. It is only in the last that it seems plausible that each contributes something that is genuinely present as the overall effect is, despite the complicated instructions for ensuring the right combined result.

Despite clear statements that contributions are not parts and that there are three distinct kinds of items when powers act, it seems that the term 'contribution' is a hostage to fortune; it keeps getting read as 'part'. Because of this, and also in deference to Machamer, Darden, and Craver's[50] insistence, long defended by Peter Machamer, that causes are active when they produce effects, I now try to be careful to talk of powers *acting*—exercising their influence on the outcome—but not about their 'contribution'.

With Machamer, I too wish to defend the place of activities in our world. A world of Humean features alone would be a strange under-populated place, devoid of so much that makes up the world that we experience. There would be no pushings; no pullings; no teachings or learnings; no smotherings or uncoverings; no eliminatings or restorings; no gratings, choppings, bakings, whiskings, sauteeings, boilings; no beheadings, invadings, executings, enslavings or freeings; no helpings nor hinderings; electings nor just taking charges. . . . I focus especially on the activities that powers engage in when they act, singly or in consort, to produce outcomes: their influencing what an outcome will be, or, following Hume's language, their 'exercising'.

---

[49] Pissarides 2007.
[50] Machamer, Darden, and Craver 2000.

Goal-directedness

It is important for the work I see powers doing that powers be *goal-directed*, as Matthew Tugby and others stress.[51] We must be careful, though, what the goal is. We should not suppose the goal of a power to be to produce as an effect something appropriately described by the label we identify the power with, like 'The goal of gravity is to produce a force $F_g = GMm/\mathbf{r}^2$'. There is a minor terminological reason for this. If we take that to be the goal of powers, then we should not label them as 'powers' in the first place because they turn out to be so utterly feeble, almost never able to achieve their goal, and in some cases even achieving the opposite.[52]

Beyond these terminological issues there is a more important point. Clever arrangements can allow a power to participate in producing almost any outcome, as in Heath Robinson or Rube Goldberg machines, where, for instance, flying a kite can sharpen a pencil or turning a ship's wheel can mix and cook pancakes. Nevertheless, there are constraints. Powers can only directly influence outcomes of a certain kind, a kind either explicitly or implicitly specified in the label we use to characterize the power. Gravity and the Coulomb power may be deployed in a Rube Goldberg machine to help cause any odd effect. But they will only do so via influencing a force. So too with all the other of the very great variety of powers at play in the analytic method. Each influences a specific kind of outcome. I propose to reserve the label 'goal' to mark this out.

For illustration, consider the earlier economics example. The first Bellman equation ($rV = -\kappa \mathbf{A} + q(J - \dot{V}) + \dot{V}$) tells us about three powers, each of which is directed towards influencing V, the value of a vacancy. The first power is associated with kA, the cost of holding a vacancy. This power 'contributes' $kA/(r-q)$ to the value of V. The second is associated with J, the value of an occupied job, and 'contributes' $qJ/(r-q)$; the third is associated with $\dot{V}$, the time derivative of the value of a vacancy, and contributes $\dot{V}/(r-q)$. Each is a different power contributing differently but all three are directed towards fixing the value of a job vacancy.

Note that here I am talking about powers and not about the independently identifiable features that the powers are associated with, which will generally, in this way of parsing the ontology, bring a number of different

---

[51] See for example Tugby 2018.
[52] As with the negative charge that, in the experimental arrangement designed by Towfic Shomar, helps cause another negative charge to move closer by exercising its power to repel. In Cartwright 1989.

powers with them. For instance, the first Bellman equation says that the quantity 'product per worker' (represented by A) in association with the multiplier k is 'the cost of holding a vacancy' and brings with it a power to influence the value of a vacancy. But, as the second Bellman equation shows, this same quantity is also supposed to bring with it a power to influence the value of an occupied job (represented by J).[53]

Powers and the need for Nature or God

I want to be careful in defending Trias powers not to promise more than I can deliver. Some powers advocates have hoped that powers by themselves would be enough to make things happen as they do, thus eliminating the need for governing laws, an occasionalist God, or Nature the artful modeler. Can we do away with all of these once we have Trias powers? I don't see how. The power of gravity is exercised in Millikan's experiment, and the drag of the air, and the Coulomb power as well. Something must fix what force actually happens when these three exercise together. In a nice case like this, the rule of vector addition may apply. But that rule is a description. It may tell us what happens, but it doesn't tell us how it happens to happen, and it certainly doesn't make things happen.

This problem is exacerbated once more features get into the act so there are no rules to go by. Even if you thought you could explain how laws of Nature make things happen without God to enforce them, that won't be enough to account for much of what happens if we ground our image of what happens in our successful scientific practices, as I urge we should. That was the lesson of Lecture 1. The array of happenings that we backread from successful scientific practice do not fall under true general propositions. The best way to recoup the facts looks to be the way we do it. That's a story about how best to learn what the facts are and about what the array of facts is like; it doesn't show how they get to be that way.[54]

---

[53] One may want to parse a powers ontology differently, so that each feature has a single power but that power can be multiply directed. I think my one-power/one-way-of-exercising picture best makes sense of scientific practice, allowing, for instance, that the same power may be associated with different features and making it clear how one power associated with a feature may be masked or finked while the others are left intact and may operate as usual.

[54] Trias powers can constrain what can happen, which is a different matter. Powers, recall, are goal-directed. Gravity affects only forces; an excited atom has a choice of lower levels to de-excite to, but that is the extent of the options being in an excited state affords it; the magnet may or may not raise the earring-back from between the floorboards, but the most it can affect is the force the earring-back experiences—it can't turn the earring-back into a pumpkin.

Some powers ontologies try to solve this problem by building into the nature of each power either the laws of combination relevant to it, or, reminiscent of Leibniz's monads, what the effects are in every arrangement it could possibly participate in with any possible powers. But if my arguments are right, there aren't enough rules for the first to work and there are too many powers and arrangements, and what they are is too open-ended, for the second. Besides, it is hard to see how this is supposed to work. How does the power of gravity, doing what it does because it is gravity, make an outcome happen that also requires Coulomb input? Similarly for the Coulombic power. It is true they do what they do together. But that does not explain *how what they produce together turns out to be just what it is*.

In defending that Nature is an artful modeler, I have argued that the facts are in accord with the designs of artful modeling of just the kind we engage in. That's description. It's deflationary, like the Mill-Ramsey-Lewis view of laws. The Spartan story of this kind of view is often found unsatisfying though: One event follows another willy-nilly; they just happen to fit the pattern described in the law claims or that of an artful modeler. So, many law advocates maintain that law claims are not just convenient summaries. The facts are as they are somehow because of the laws the claims represent. But it is notoriously difficult to explain how this can be if there is no God to write the laws, no Great Book to write them in, and no enforcer to make the facts toe the line. You may wonder why I have gone in for the image of Nature designing the world much as we design the Oxford knee. It is in part to underline my quarrel with the concept of *laws of nature*, not just with its failure to fit the facts but with the very idea of a *law* that can dictate what should happen. We have grown used to using the concept despite not knowing how to make good on it, averting our gaze, as with the problem of induction. But Governing Laws are just as much a metaphor as Nature the Modeler, and, as I urged in Lecture 1, not such an apt one.

So Trias powers ontology cannot, any more than any other account I know of, tell us what makes things happen as they do, though Trias powers will be part of that story. They do another job. They make sense of some of our most valued scientific practices.

1. ii Probabilistic Causality

Besides the analytic method, exercisings/influencings also appear in our treatment of probabilistic powers: ones that do not always exercise whenever they are present and properly triggered. Consider radioactivity. A carbon-14 atom may sit for a long time, then suddenly its power to emit a beta particle is exercised. There is, contra Hume, a difference between the obtaining of this power[55] and its exercise.

This difference matters when it comes to practical methodology. Probabilistic powers are often taken to raise problems for one of our standard assumptions about the relations between causality and probability: the *causal Markov condition*, which says that once we have controlled for the causes that produce a feature, that feature will not be correlated with anything but its own effects. This principle is widely used for causal inference in both the natural and social sciences. It is at the heart of both genuinely controlled experiments and experiments where 'control' is mimicked by random assignment—the randomized controlled trials so central in medicine and increasingly across the social sciences. Carbon-14 provides an example of the problems that the causal Markov condition faces when causes are probabilistic. A carbon-14 atom will emit a beta particle just in case it emits an electron anti-neutrino—which is part of the evidence that lepton number is a conserved quantity. Suppose we have controlled for the presence of the carbon-14 atom, which we suppose in a particular situation to be the sole cause of beta particles. Still, the presence of the beta particle is correlated with the presence of the electron anti-neutrino even though the electron anti-neutrino is not among its causes.

This problem is not really with the causal Markov condition. Rather, I have not been faithful to the spirit of the principle in the interpretation I used of it. So far, following the standard interpretation, I have been too Humean. The idea behind the causal Markov principle is that once everything is fixed about the bringing about of a feature, then the feature won't be correlated with anything but its own effects. But the presence of the carbon-14 isn't all that's needed to bring about the beta particle; the power to produce a beta particle has to exercise as well. And once we fix whether this exercising has happened or not, the beta particle will no longer be correlated with the presence of an electron anti-neutrino.

This case also illustrates one way we can have evidence that a power has exercised over and above the occurrence of its effect. Here the power to produce a beta particle influences the occurrence of a beta particle if and only if another power of carbon-14 is exercised, this one to produce an electron anti-neutrino. So, the exercising of the beta-emitting power leaves

---

[55] Or, where relevant, of the power plus its trigger.

a measurable trace beyond the beta particle itself—indeed not one trace but two. The carbon-14 is itself changed by exercising these two powers, into a nitrogen atom, which we can also observe by independent means.

1. iii Post Hoc Evaluation

Evaluation and assessment is a big field nowadays, essential, for example, in cases of 'payment by results'. As an illustration: the American Psychological Association lists sixteen journals with *Evaluation* or *Assessment* in their title in a list they have compiled of "Journals in Assessment, Evaluation, Measurement, Psychometrics and Statistics" (2018).

Evaluation studies try to answer the question, 'Did—or did not—this specific policy produce its intended outcome.' Consider the UK government's *Teen-Age Pregnancy Strategy*, which was actively implemented across UK governments for the past fifteen years. The rate of conceptions among under-18s in the UK dropped from 41.6 per 1,000 girls in that age-group in 2007 to 22.9 per 1,000 in 2014. Did the Strategy play a central role? Note that there is no doubt that the drop in pregnancies occurred, nor that the Strategy could have played a central role, nor that other changes occurred that might have been chiefly responsible instead (or as well)—like young people spending less time together and far more at home (a couple of hours each day) on social media, or a general change in attitude, the so-called 'generation sensible' (today's UK teenagers are also less likely to drink, smoke, and take drugs). Did the UK's Teen-Age Pregnancy Strategy actually have a major influence? The whole field of evaluation makes sense only if we think there is an answer to this kind of question.

Jennifer McKitrick has criticized Trias ontologies.[56] One of her concerns is about what empirical evidence there is in favor of exercisings by contrast with evidence for effects. Evaluators have the same concern, only at a practical level. They are very alert to the fallacy of *post hoc, ergo propter hoc*. They don't look just to see if the policy was properly implemented and then the effect occurred later; they want to know if the policy genuinely influenced the outcome. So, we may look to evaluation studies to see what kinds of evidence are typically adduced. This is what I've been doing in the last while and I've come up with a category scheme. I think you will find these altogether familiar and obvious, which is all to the good from my point of

---

[56] McKitrick 2010.

view since I claim that, though it is not explicit, the assumption and use of powers and their influence on effects is endemic in scientific practice. The first divide is between *direct* and *indirect* evidence.

Direct evidence looks at aspects of the power, the effect, and how the power is supposed to influence that effect; *indirect*, at features outside these that bear on whether the power influenced the effect.

The prominent kind of *indirect evidence*[57] is evidence that helps eliminate alternatives. Alexander Bird (2010, 345) calls this 'Holmesian inference' because of the famous Sherlock Holmes remark that when all other possibilities have been eliminated, what remains must be responsible even if improbable. The idea here is to calculate what the observed effect would be given all other powers that exercised; if that's different from the actually observed effect, the only explanation is that the power in question influenced the outcome. If we have a good enough understanding of the other powers, we can do this directly. But even when we don't, we can still get relevant evidence. Suppose, for instance, that we had enrolled all the teenage girls in the UK in a well conducted randomized controlled trial that subjected half of them to the Teen-Age Pregnancy Strategy and withheld it from the other half. We could then estimate the average difference that the Strategy made to the girls in the trial, regardless of what other factors influenced the outcomes.

Direct evidence that a power influenced an outcome can be thought of under six headings:

- *Characteristics of the effect*. Does the effect occur at the time, in the manner, and of the size to be expected had the power helped produce it? It takes time for most powers to exercise. If the effect occurs too soon or too late, the power couldn't have contributed to it. Or the effect may be too big or too small given what we know about the possible influence of other factors. Or, suppose the effect is strongest where the power occurred less often, for instance, where the Teenage Pregnancy Strategy was poorly implemented and didn't reach many recipients. That would count against its having helped significantly.
- *Symptoms that the power has exercised*. We have seen examples of this in the discussion of probabilistic causality but they serve equally as evidence in cases where a power always exercises when properly triggered. For instance,

---

[57] Indirect evidence—eliminating all plausible alternatives—is what constitutes *rigor* according to Julian Reiss (2015, 156).

the power itself may change in predictable ways when it exercises; or it may exercise in correlation with another power so that finding evidence of the effects of one power constitutes evidence for the exercising of the other.
- *Support factors.* Some powers can only exercise in the presence of other specific features—so-called 'support factors', as in our well-worn philosophical example: Striking a match produces fire only in the presence of oxygen. Finding necessary support factors absent shows the power couldn't have contributed. Finding them present is some evidence in favor.
- *Triggers.* Their presence or absence can be strong evidence, depending on how necessary they are to get the power to exercise and how reliable they are at it.
- *Masks, finks, anti-dotes, spoilers, interferences*—anything that can stop the exercising of a power in its tracks or undo it before it influences the effect. Their presence can be strong evidence against the power's contributing, depending on how reliable they are. Their absence is some evidence that the power exercised and influenced the effect.
- *Intermediaries.* A very great many of the powers we study are derivative. They depend on concatenating the exercise of subsidiary powers across time and space. Evidence that the intermediate powers or their effects occurred and exercised or not (and at the time, manner and size required) doubles as evidence for or against the derivative powers' claim to have influenced the outcome. Consider the 'worm wars' that followed a reanalysis of the data from Ted Miguel and Michael Kremer's Kenyan study[58] of the effects of deworming on children's educational outcomes. One discussion[59] explains that the effects on educational outcomes were supposed to be brought about by intermediate effects on health outcomes: Children without worms are healthy enough to come to school, are better nourished, and have improved learning aptitude. It then claims that the data support a correlation between the deworming and educational outcomes (though that may be spurious due to weaknesses in the study design) but not between deworming and the mediating health outcomes. This lack of correlation is evidence that the deworming did not contribute to improved educational outcomes even if these outcomes obtained.

So, evaluation studies are yet another practice that best makes sense if we suppose an ontology of Trias powers.

---

[58] Miguel and Kramer 2004.
[59] Humphreys 2015.

2. Powers, Conditionals, Symbolic Representations, and Doing It by the Book

Powers have gotten themselves into some bad company, and I've helped them into it. The bad company is conditionals. As Florian Fisher notes, "Dispositions are related to conditionals, or as Elizabeth Prior puts it: 'What is commonly accepted by all those who discuss dispositions[60] is that there exists a conceptual connection between a statement attributing a disposition to an item and a particular conditional. The acceptance of the existence of this conceptual connection is a pre-theoretic common ground' [Prior, 1985, 5]. Now, virtually nobody would challenge the connection between dispositional statements and the corresponding conditional statements . . ."[61] But, he adds that that does not imply that disposition ascriptions have to be analyzed via conditionals. Similarly, John Heil proposes, "conditionals provide a defeasible, rough and ready way to pick out dispositions."[62]

Even if conditionals are not to serve as an analysis, and even if they do their job defeasibly, I disagree not only with the need for any particular conditionals to be associated with a disposition but with the possibility of them, at least in so far as powers count as dispositions. That is for both metaphysical and philosophy of science reasons.

Metaphysically, what do powers need conditionals for? Powers are no more latent or in need of conditionals to give sense to them than anything else. Powers may not be exercising all the time, but they are there or they are not there independent of whether they exercise. And the nice things for us is that science has learned, for many powers, a variety of ways to recognize that they are there—ways of observing them, measuring them—independent of waiting for observations of outcomes they are supposed to influence.

From a philosophy of science point of view, we have trouble finding something to put in the consequent of these conditionals. That's what I had hoped 'contribution' would do. But that doesn't work. We need three elements in our powers ontology, but the third is an activity: Powers only influence outcomes when they exercise. This is not the kind of thing to appear in the consequent of a conditional. Gravity may pull objects and

---

[60] This includes Alexander Bird, whose views on dispotions and laws are discussed in chapter 7.
[61] Fischer 2018, 38
[62] Heil 2005, 345. Both Fischer and Heil note that this does not mean that the conditional constitutes an analysis.

resistors may resist the flow of electricity—those are activities. But what could it mean to say that when it exercises, gravity pulls Gmm/$\mathbf{r}^2$-ly or the resistor, when it exercises, resists 4 Ohms-ly? I can't figure out what kind of thing 'resisting 4 Ohms-ly' could refer to should it appear in the consequent of a conditional. Rather than endorse conditionals with ill-defined consequents, it seems more honest to adopt the view I defend here, that powers act and these canonical descriptions serve not as consequents of conditionals but as labels that we know how to use to calculate overall effects when the act.

We do see a conditional for the power of gravity in my caricature Millikan theory. But I have argued that the expression in the consequent there does not refer. There are no component forces in addition to the overall force. What then of the formula, $F_G = GMm/\mathbf{r}^2$? I repeat: This formula

- tells us that there is a power (dubbed 'the power of gravity) that influences the force on a body of mass m located **r** away, and
- associates a label to this power, 'GMm/$\mathbf{r}^2$' that we know how to deploy in calculating what happens, generally very effectively.

'$F_G = GMm/\mathbf{r}^2$' is, like the laws I discussed in Lecture 1, a *symbolic representation*. This is even more clear once we move to other cases. The label '4 ohms' on a speaker allows us to calculate the current when the speaker is inserted into a variety of circuits. But it doesn't naturally lend itself to some simple conditionals that help identify it.

If we want to endorse a Trias powers ontology, we must of course be able to say a lot about what powers and their exercisings are and how they work—to give a thick account of them. Otherwise our talk is empty; we have only what McKitrick calls an "I know not what."[63] But we do not have that. We know a reasonable amount about Trias powers in the abstract, including the features I have described:

- Powers can be labeled by individual symbolic representations.
- We know how to use these labels to predict and manipulate the world.
- For some arrangements of powers (as in Millikan's oil drop experiment), we have articulated rules for how to predict what happens when powers act together, and our predictions are often both very precise and very accurate.

---

[63] McKitrick 2010, 83.

- These are generally highly controlled arrangements where only powers all studied in the same theoretical domain significantly influence the outcome. As I reported in Lecture 1, we have very few cross-domain rules of composition.
- For many other arrangements, we have rules of thumb, which again we often use with great success.
- There are empirically confirmable correlations between a particular power and other independently identifiable features, for example, between having a (gravitational) mass M and having the power labeled '$F_G = GMm/r^2$'.
- Powers can often be represented with very precise mathematical formulae.
- There is a distinction between the presence of a power and its exercising, which is apparent in powers that need triggering or powers that exercise only some of the time, as in purely probabilistic powers.
- There is a distinction between the exercising of a power and the overall effect it helps produce.

More important, the Trias ontology is grounded in empirical reality, and in two ways. It gets its evidence from the successes of our scientific methods; and we know a very great deal about a very great many specific powers and how they combine; the examples in boxes 2.1 to 2.6 point to only an infinitesimal fraction of this knowledge.

We can, and do, use our knowledge about powers to generate conditionals. But that is true of much of our knowledge. There is no "corresponding" conditional for each power, no "conceptual connection between a statement attributing a disposition to an item and a particular conditional"—and there is no need for them. Powers are a basic part of the ontology of the scientific image and they are well supported empirically.

3. Contingency

3. i Powers and the Varieties of Contingency

On a Trias powers account, contingency can arise along three axes: in the *nature of the powers* themselves; in the *rules of combination* when powers act together; and in the effects of arrangement on what happens.[64]

---

[64] These are relevant to standard accounts of laws of nature as well. See Cartwright and Merlussi 2016, which is chapter 6 in the present volume.

- *The nature of a power.* Powers may have three different modes of acting. First, a power has one and only one way of influencing an outcome to which it is goal-directed. No *permissiveness* here. Second, there is a set of available ways of influencing the outcome and a probability over these. The power must act in accord with these probabilities. Third, the power may have an available set of ways of exercising but no constraints on how often it exercises in one way or the other, even in the long run. Quantum theory commits us to permissiveness in the second sense. Once we are on board with quantum theory, the only remaining issue is whether we are insistent that, despite appearances, everything else is really deterministic in some God's-eye view or we are happy to allow that things may be much as we experience them, permissive in both the second and third senses.
- *Rules of combination.* The familiar rule of vector addition fixes a single force that results in arrangements where two sources of force act together. But we can imagine *permissive* rules that allow a range of outcomes, either with or without a probability over them.
- *The effects of the arrangement.* Of course the effects of the arrangement are already there in the rules of combination. Consider vector addition. For a resultant, say $GMm/\mathbf{r}^2 \oplus \varepsilon q_1 q_2/\mathbf{r'}^2$, to represent the force an object experiences, the object with the gravitational power $GMm/\mathbf{r}^2$ must be located at the position $\mathbf{r}$ away from it, the object with the Coulomb power $\varepsilon q_1 q_2/\mathbf{r'}^2$ must be located $\mathbf{r'}$ from it, and there must be no other powers operating to influence the force on it.

Arrangements are a different source of contingency from rules of combination because, for most situations, rules of combination will not cover all the aspects that are relevant to what happens. These are cases where, as I argued in Lecture 1, Nature, like us, acts as an artful modeler. Recall the example of the Santa Cruz Island foxes where at the very best the Nature Conservancy had some rules of thumb, rough-and-ready regularities, and analogies to guide them. There's no evidence that Nature had more. She does not follow the rules of combination because there aren't any. Yet she does something sensible, just as we do when we construct our predictive models. This is a far more radical kind of permissiveness than those above since here what happens seems constrained not to any fixed set of outcomes but only by Nature's good efforts to make the world reasonably intelligible for us.

3. ii Whence Possibility in the Natural World?[65]

David Lewis thought other possible worlds were real; that gives us the best account of modality and counterfactuals (as well as of verisimilitude, knowledge, belief, and desire). Willard van Orman Quine[66] scoffed at possibility: How many possible fat men are there in that doorway and what are they like? Suppose the domain of quantification is men. The Barcan formulae prescribe that $\Diamond \exists x(x$ is fat now & x is in the doorway now) iff $\exists x \Diamond (x$ is fat now & x is in the doorway now). These formulae are due to my teacher Ruth Barcan Marcus.[67] Marcus believed in possibilia, but possibilia that are based in the objects and facts of the actual world—the only world there is. I follow her here. So whence possibilia? They are a natural consequence of permissive powers, which, I have argued, we are committed to if we embrace quantum theory. More radically, they are also a consequence of permissive arrangements, where even Nature has no rules to go by.

Think about those possible fat men in the doorway. How many are there at this moment? That depends on when the possibilities are assessed. What is possible now was different at different times in the past. Two minutes ago there weren't many. Principally because there weren't many fat men in the vicinity then, and the kinds of powers that affect men's weights do not include any that permit fast weight gain in these circumstances. Suppose there were a few fat men here then. It is likely they have the power of locomotion, which is a very permissive power: to stay in one place or move in any direction at a range of speeds, and with no probability over those outcomes.[68] And the arrangements that the power of locomotion for those fat men seem equally permissive, though it may be a little inhibiting that they would have to get up and move about in the middle of a lecture. So how many possible fat men in the doorway now were there two minutes ago and what are their characteristics? That has an answer, though I don't know it. It depends on how far which men are located from the door and whether the range of their locomotive powers included walking fast enough to get there in time.

---

[65] I only discuss here natural possibility, and not, for instance 'theoretical' possibility—what theory would allow were it true, nor logical possibility, nor, if there is such a thing, metaphysical possibility.

[66] Quine 1948.

[67] Marcus 1975-1976.

[68] If there are probabilities for the outcomes it looks as if they reside in the triggers for locomotion.

Marcus tells us, "An actual chess player in an actual game has alternative moves of which he selects one. . . . it is difficult to deny such unactualized moves an objective status. The alternatives can be precisely described and many of their immediate consequences traced. Such examples can be multiplied. Alternative experimental outcomes, partially completed projects, 'generate' possibilia of great specificity. They are not merely in the mind or vagaries of fancy. They present themselves publicly and are clearly identifiable."[69]

I picked this passage because here Marcus provides concrete examples: possible moves in a chess game, possible outcomes of an experiment, the possible outcomes of a project—close to my interest in the possible outcomes of a policy intervention. I am struck, looking back on the passage, that her examples are all paradigms of how I picture possibilities to be generated. There are various systems, like chess pieces, with specific powers arrayed in particular arrangements. What is possible in the future depends in one fell swoop on the powers of the parts, their arrangements, and any fixed rules about how the powers combine. Each piece in a chess game has the power to stay still or to move, and if they are to exercise their power to move, a set of possible moves is fixed—subject to the arrangement—with no probabilities over them. The nature of their powers, the rules, and the specific arrangement at any time fix what is next possible. Except in castling, only one power can be exercised at a time, and the arrangement and the rules fix which can and which cannot be exercised. But the game is designed to admit a wide range of possibilities. Much of the time there is considerable choice about which powers to trigger and how they will exercise.

Experiments are just opposite. In an experiment, we generally wish to design an arrangement in which the inputs and their consequent effects are so tightly constrained that the only outputs possible teach us what we want to know. Often the skill of this is in engineering the set-up so that the only features relevant to producing outcomes are ones for which there are rules of combination, so what happens can be predicted with relative certainty.

The lesson here is that, whether the future possibilities in a given situation are wide open, or, conversely, they are narrowly constrained, what those possibilities are is fixed by:

---

[69] Marcus 1975-1976, 43.

- What kinds of powers are present
- How they are arranged
- What can happen when they act together in whatever ways they can in that arrangement.

I began with the truism that where there are no rules to dictate, Nature is on her own. And I have argued that this is much of the time, because:

- Many powers are permissive.
- Rules of combination may be so too.
- Most rules of combination fix what happens only where powers from one specific domain alone influence what happens—as in Millikan's experiment where nothing significantly affects the acceleration of the oil drop except what can properly be represented as a force.

The third is what's really new, by comparison with a world that evolves in accord with laws of nature. It is a consequence of the fact that neither we nor Nature can do it by the book. Situations where the 'Nothing-else' rider can be ignored are few and far between. In fact, these are even fewer and farther between than we like to let on. Millikan notoriously threw out data points on the grounds that something or other affected those outcomes that he had no way to handle within the rules. After twenty years in the making and the tightest controls imaginable at every stage, only three of the four gyroscopes in the Stanford Gravity Probe worked according to plan.

In Sum

Nature the artful modeler creates a world with pockets of highly predictable order, large swathes of happenings we can predict more or less accurately, and ones we haven't a clue about, a world where our plans for wonderful new devices and policies work some of the time, as with the Oxford knee and the evacuation of Fort McMurray, and some of the time go dramatically wrong, as with the opening-day oscillations of the London Millennium Bridge or the failure of the O rings on the *Challenger* space shuttle. She does it that way because she must. This is what comes naturally once we get out of our theories and into the real embodied world with its endless array of powers and arrangements. And it is a world just like the one we actually observe. The cussedness of machines is not a freak of Meccano building or of auto repair. It is our universal experience. That, for an empiricist, should be good reason to suppose that that is the very world we live in.

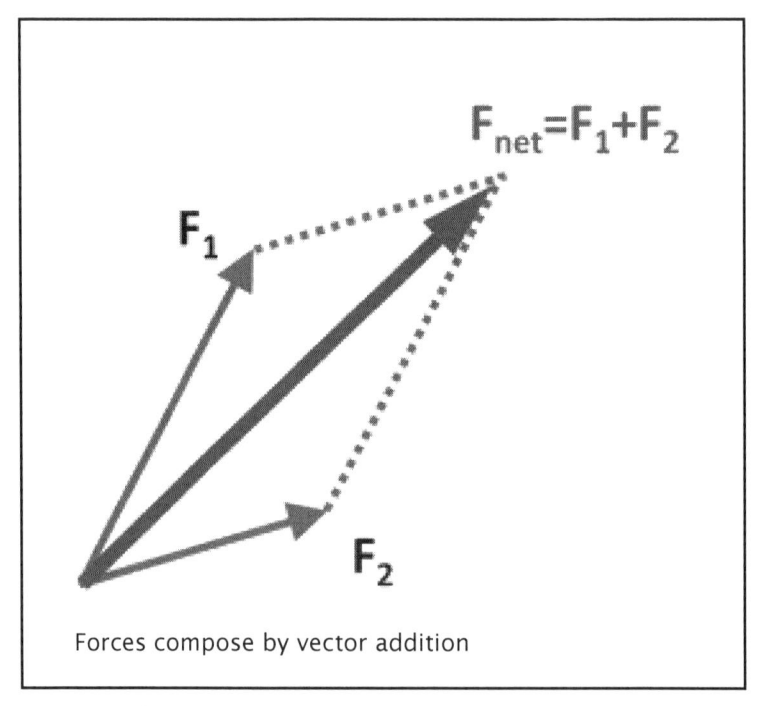

$F_{net}=F_1+F_2$

Forces compose by vector addition

Box 2.1 Combining Forces. Figure by Brews Ohare.

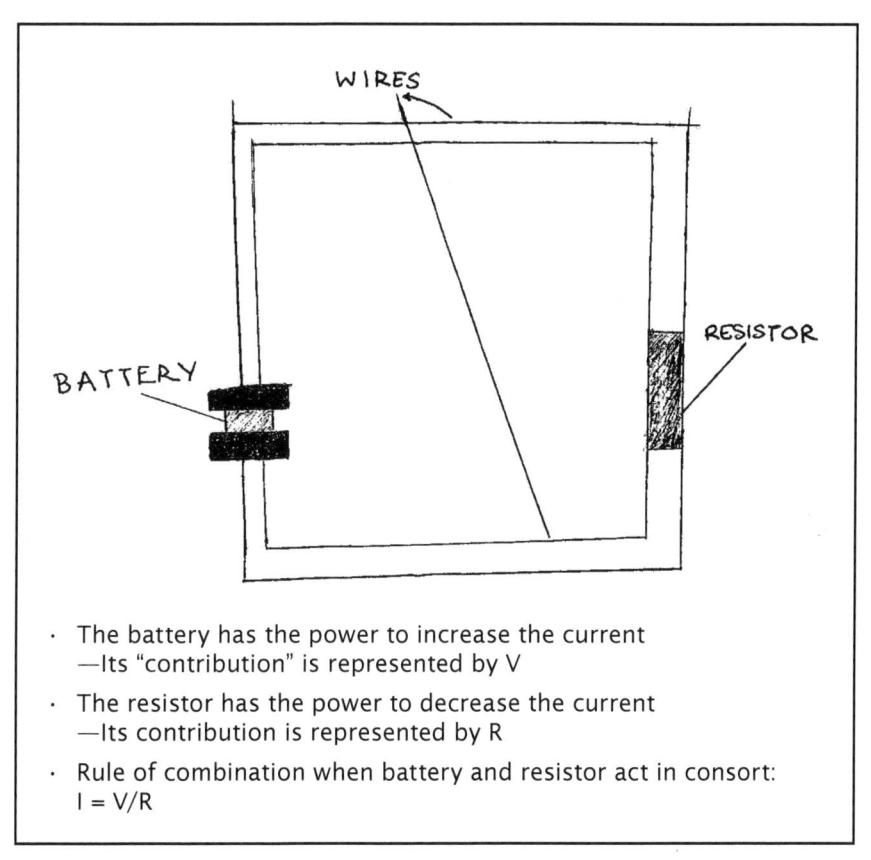

- The battery has the power to increase the current
  —Its "contribution" is represented by V
- The resistor has the power to decrease the current
  —Its contribution is represented by R
- Rule of combination when battery and resistor act in consort:
  I = V/R

Box 2.2 Combining "Contributions" in Simple Circuits. Drawing by Lucy Charlton.

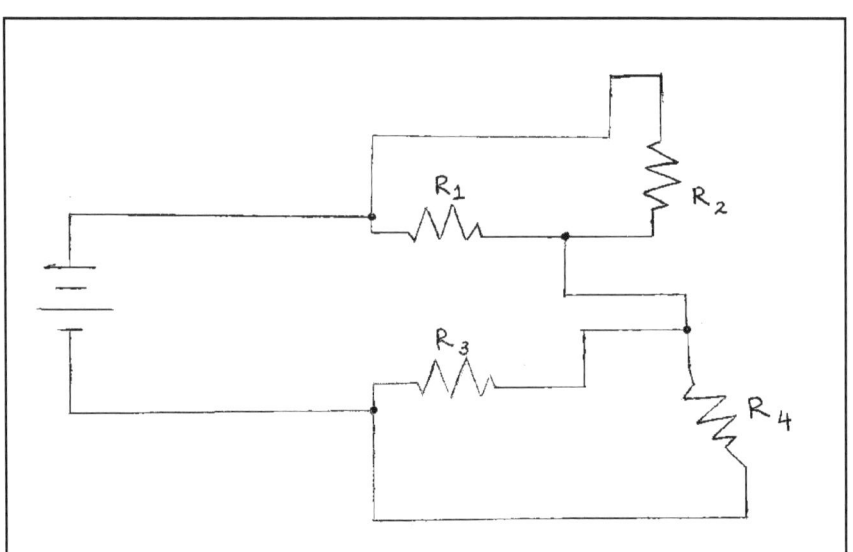

To simplify a convoluted circuit schematic, follow these steps: Trace current from one side of the battery to the other, following any single path ("loop") to the battery. Sometimes it works better to start with the loop containing the most components, but regardless of the path taken the result will be accurate. Mark polarity of voltage drops across each resistor as you trace the loop. Draw those components you encounter along this loop in a vertical schematic.

Mark traced components in the original diagram and trace remaining loops of components in the circuit. Use polarity marks across traced components as guides for what connects where. Document new components in loops on the vertical re-draw schematic as well.

Repeat last step as often as needed until all components in original diagram have been traced.

Box 2.3 Combining in Complex Circuits. Drawing by Lucy Charlton. Text from Tony R. Kuphaldt, *Lessons in Electric Circuits*, vol. 1, 5th ed., 2006, 216.

Nature's Raw Materials

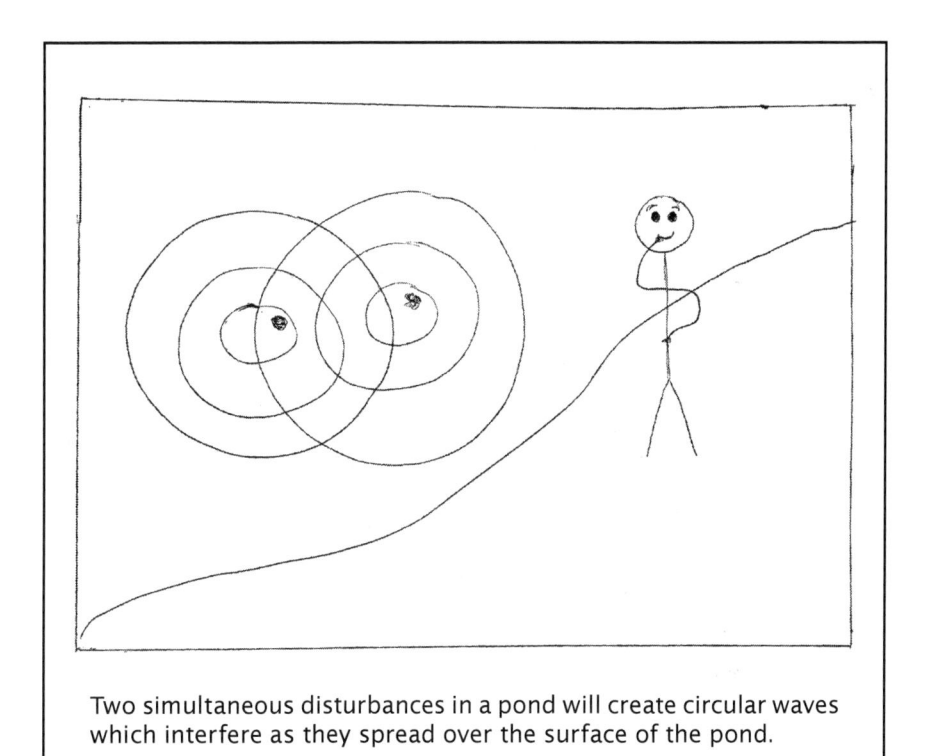

> Two simultaneous disturbances in a pond will create circular waves which interfere as they spread over the surface of the pond.

Box 2.4 Combining Waves. Drawing by Lucy Charlton.

> ### 5. Insecticides Acting Together
>
> To analyze the joint action of two (or more) insecticides, the actual toxicity indexes of the components and their mixture are determined by dosage-mortality curves. The theoretical toxicity of the same mixture is equal to the sum of toxicity indexes calculated from the percentage of each component times its respective toxicity index. Therefore, the joint toxicity or Co-toxicity coefficient of a mixture A coefficient of a mixture near 100 indicates probability of a similar action; independent action usually should give a coefficient less than 100, while a coefficient significantly above 100 strongly indicates synergism. Toxicity significantly less than that of the strongest toxicant alone shows antagonism.

Box 2.5 Insecticides Acting Together. From "Analysis of Joint Action of Insecticides Against House Flies," Yun-Pei Sun and E. R. Johnson, *Journal of Economic Entomology* 53, no. 5, (October 1960): 887.

> ### 6. Sounds Acting Together
>
> Ensemble musicians coordinate their actions with remarkable precision. The ensemble cohesion that results is predicated upon group members sharing a common goal; a unified concept of the ideal sound. The current chapter reviews research addressing three cognitive processes that enable individuals to realize such shared goals while engaged in musical joint action. The first process is auditory imagery; specifically, anticipating one's own sounds and the sounds produced by other performers. The second process, prioritized integrative attention, involves dividing attention between one's own actions (high priority) and those of others (lower priority) while monitoring the overall, integrated ensemble sound. The third process relates to adaptive timing, i.e., adjusting the timing of one's movements in order to maintain synchrony in the face of tempo changes and other, often unpredictable events.

Box 2.6 Sounds Acting Together. From "Joint Action in Music Performance," Peter E. Keller, in *Enacting Intersubjectivity: A Cognitive and Social Perspective on the Study of Interactions*, ed. F. Morganti, A. Carassa, G. Riva, Amsterdam: IOS Press, 2008, 201.

3

Nature's Limits

Picking up where Nature leaves off, building it better, and warranting your work.

Introduction

Lecture 3 is an exercise in what I have dubbed *the philosophy of social technology*, which studies how to build more decent societies. It is a special subfield of philosophy not just because of its subject matter but also because it lies at the intersection of other more established fields which it needs to call on for help, especially philosophy of science,[70] political philosophy, and ethics. My own work in this field has been primarily on the philosophy of science side, using work on evidence, objectivity, and causal modeling to think about how to ensure our social policy outcomes are what we hope for. Much of this work has focused on developing better concepts of evidence in the context of the widespread and highly influential evidence-based policy (EBP) movement, with its many What Works sites[71] that review research results on policy effectiveness.

To this end, it is useful to distinguish two approaches to predicting policy effectiveness in situ, the *intervention-centered* and the *context-centered*. I argue that we need to put far more effort into the context-centered. You will not be surprised at that once I tell you that the context-centered approach employs artful modeling. The intervention-centered is a special case. Its success generally depends on what Michael Strevens calls 'Voodoo that works'.[72]

---

[70] This includes natural, social, and decision sciences.
[71] Like the US Department of Education's What Works Clearing House, the Abdul Latif Jameel Poverty Action Lab (J-PAL, heavily staffed by MIT economists), the ten official UK What Works Centres, or Conservation Evidence, which I mention below.
[72] Strevens 2012.

This is another case, like the three discussed in Lecture 2, where a Trias powers ontology makes sense of scientific practice, in this case practices that predict policy outcomes. It is the principal reason I have returned these many years later to the work I started on powers in the late 1980s. I hope to make clear the role that Trias powers play, and especially the importance of arrangements. But I am not going to present it primarily that way because I believe that the considerations I raise are of relevance both practically and philosophically whether or not they are underpinned by powers.

There are three problems about how policies achieve their results that the intervention-centered approach falls foul of.

1. The *problem of the long view*. Nature takes short views. The kinds of outcomes we look for from our interventions are seldom in the remit of the powers the interventions bring. Nature produces these outcomes through intermediate stages, not in one fell swoop. What then secures the policy/outcome pairings that are at the heart of the intervention-centered approach?
2. The *Donald Davidson problem*. The event reported on page 1 column 2 of the *New York Times* can influence that described on page 5, column 1, but not under those descriptions. Similarly with the steps in the policy process as we describe them.
3. The *concatenation problem*. However the causal process connecting policy with outcome is divided into stages, the effect of stage n must be a cause in stage n + 1. This depends not on the policy and its powers but on the arrangement in which these powers exercise.

I'll discuss these in section 2; section 3 explains why context matters; section 4, when we can get away with the intervention-centering despite this; section 5 shows how intervention-centering makes use of Strevens's voodoo; section 6 shows how difficult context modeling is, looking back to Lecture 1. I conclude extremely briefly with the reminder that our troubles here are not of our own making. We must be artful modelers because that's what Nature is.

1. The Two Approaches

Both approaches aim to help policy makers pick policies that are reasonably likely to achieve their targeted outcomes. The *intervention-centered approach* focuses on features of the policies themselves, in particular, on whether they 'work'. It has the admirable goal of learning from experience:

Find out what has worked elsewhere as a guide to what to do here. Much of the effort in evidence-based policy goes into accumulating and vetting evidence that the policy has worked elsewhere; and to broaden this evidence base and to make it more secure, policy makers are urged to implement policies in ways that allow their success or failure to be documented rigorously. The *context-centered approach* focuses on the context where policies are to be implemented, in particular, on understanding what kinds of causal pathways to the targeted outcome it affords.

Box 3.1 highlights some of the central features of each.

The Intervention-centered Approach to Policy Choice

1. Focuses: on characteristics of the policy.
    - Does it work?
    - For whom, when, and where?
    - What does it take to implement it?
    - How much does it cost?
    - What are the side effects?
2. Studies:
    - Repeatable causal processes
    - Measurable outcomes.
3. Requires: evidence strong enough to support generalization or transfer of policy outcomes.

The Context-centered Approach to Policy Choice

1. Focuses: on the arrangements in the target context.
2. Studies: what causal processes these afford; what changes can be made in the arrangements so that they afford more desirable processes.
3. Requires:
    - A model of what's happening in the target context
    - An understanding of how the arrangements and powers exercising there afford this
    - A plan to change what's happening, via producing either
    - A new intervention, old structure
        ◦ New structure
        ◦ Evidence for all of this.

Box 3.1

58   *Nancy Cartwright*

The evaluation literature sometimes distinguishes studies of the 'causes of effects' from studies of the 'effects of causes'. The intervention/context distinction is related but is not the same. Both approaches are concerned to identify what the causes might be of targeted effects. The difference is in how they expect to find these. The intervention-centered hopes to do so by identifying some causes that can generally be relied on to produce those effects across different contexts. The context-centered, by identifying what causal pathways to the effect are locally possible.

As just one of thousands and thousands of examples of intervention-centered practice, consider a typical passage from the 'Quick Guide'... *Learning from Research: Systematic Reviews for Informing Policy Decisions,* published by a typical institution[73] that specializes in, as their website reports "(i) developing methods for systematic reviewing and synthesis of research evidence; and (ii) developing methods for the study of the use research."[74]

> Each concept within the question has to be carefully defined, as this will affect which studies are included or excluded... Thus a review on the effects of homework on children would require clarity of what was meant by both '*children*' and '*homework*', and also what '*effects*' were to be considered.[75]

The focus on the careful definition of cause and effect suggests that there is supposed to be something 'internal' to the cause with respect to that effect, or as I would say, that the policy has a 'goal-directed' power towards that effect. But that seems unlikely. Look, for example, at Figure 3.1, taken from the book and the website[76] published by *Conservation Evidence* (n.b., not the Nature Conservancy that I discussed in Lecture 1).[77]

I hoped for information about breeding foxes and other Canidaes in captivity; but they don't do mammals, so I have copied out part of their report on birds. I wanted to look at foxes because I have already described the suc-

---

[73] The EPPI Centre (Evidence for Policy and Practice Information and Co-ordinating Centre) at University College, London. The publication is authored by David Gough, Sandy Oliver, and James Thomas, 2013.
[74] Social Science Research Unit, UCL Institute of Education 2016.
[75] Social Science Research Unit, UCL Institute of Education 2016, 12.
[76] Sutherland et al. 2015.
[77] According to their website, "*Conservation Evidence is a free, authoritative information resource designed to support decisions about how to maintain and restore global biodiversity.* We summarise evidence from the scientific literature about the effects of conservation interventions such as methods of habitat or species management. Expert panels are then asked to assess the effectiveness (or not) of interventions, based on the summarized evidence ..." [original emphasis]. Sutherland et al. 2015.

3.15.1 Captive breeding		
Based on the collated evidence, what is the current assessment of the effectiveness of interventions for captive breeding?		
Likely to be beneficial	• Artificially incubate and hand-rear birds in captivity: raptors • Artificially incubate and hand-rear birds in captivity: seabirds • Artificially incubate and hand-rear birds in captivity: songbirds • Artificially incubate and hand-rear birds in captivity: waders • Use captive breeding to increase or maintain population raptors	
Unknown effectiveness (limited evidence)	• Artificially incubate and hand-rear birds in captivity: bustards • Artificially incubate and hand-rear birds in captivity: cranes • Artificially incubate and hand-rear birds in captivity: gamebirds • Artificially incubate and hand-rear birds in captivity: parrots	

□ Use captive breeding to increase or maintain populations of storks and ibises
  ○ Unknown effectiveness (limited evidence) | Based on: 4 studies

□ Use captive breeding to increase or maintain populations of raptors
  • Likely to be beneficial | Based on: 5 studies

□ Use captive breeding to increase or maintain populations of bustards
  ○ Unknown effectiveness (limited evidence) | Based on: 4 studies

□ Use artificial insemination in captive breeding
  ○ Unknown effectiveness (limited evidence) | Based on: 5 studies

□ Use captive breeding to increase or maintain populations of pigeons
  ○ Unknown effectiveness (limited evidence) | Based on: 1 study

□ Use captive breeding to increase or maintain populations of songbirds
  ○ Unknown effectiveness (limited evidence) | Based on: 3 studies

□ Artificially incubate and hand-rear bustards in captivity
  ○ Unknown effectiveness (limited evidence) | Based on: 2 studies

Figure 3.1 From *What Works in Conservation*, ed. W. J. Sutherland, L. V. Dicks, N. Ockendon, and R. K. Smith. Cambridge: Open Book Publishers, 2015. http://dx.doi.org/10.11647/OBP.006 on the left, and on the right, from conservationevidence.com/data/index?terms=raptors&yt1=

cessful intervention to save the Santa Cruz Island foxes in Lecture 1, which included *breeding in captivity*. Given the complexity of the intervention and the complexity of the ecology where it was delivered, was the Santa Cruz success really due to the exercise of the power of protected breeding sites to improve fox numbers?

Let's turn to my three serious arguments to back up my skepticism about this power.

2. The Three Problems

2. i The Long View Problem

This arises because of the gap in time between policy implementation and outcome. Few outcomes of policy interest are achieved directly by the policy features but rather through a series of intermediate stages. These are described in what the evaluation literature calls the *theory of change* of the policy, where the causally relevant features of the intermediate steps are represented by what are called *mediator variables*. The outcome will only be achieved if the causally relevant features at each step have the power to influence the causally relevant features at the next.

We can suppose that the policy features are goal directed, as the Trias powers ontology teaches. But if the outcome is to occur, they must be directed towards getting the very first step in the process in place, not the ultimate outcome. After that the features that appear at subsequent steps take over, each in turn. The outcome is achieved not because the policy has a power that is goal-directed to influencing it but only if the policy has the power to kick off the process correctly. Recall my short discussion of the worm wars in Lecture 2. Giving children deworming pills *may* increase their reading scores in some contexts. But if so, that is not because deworming pills have the power to influence how well one reads but because, for instance, in the children's guts they have the power to interfere with the proteins in the worms' intestine or absorptive cells, which has the power to inhibit the worms' ability to absorb sugars, which can starve them of energy, which can kill the worms, which can make the children worm free, which in that context can (thinking in bigger steps) . . . influence the health of the children, which in turn has the power to influence their school attendance and their ability to think, which in turn, acting in consort, has the power to improve their ability to read—as the theory of change for this policy suggests.

2. ii The Donald-Davidson Problem

Consider the Rube Goldberg pencil sharpener, which I use again and again as I see more and more lessons coming from it.[78] With this machine in hand, it is a very effective policy to fly a kite outside the study window in order to sharpen pencils. We can understand why by taking short views. Flying the kite opens the door of a little cage, opening the door of the cage frees some moths, the freed moths eat some flannel sitting on a plate, the disappearance of the flannel lightens the weight on the plate . . ., eventually, the pecking of the woodpecker sharpens the pencil.

But flying kites does not usually influence cage door opening, any more than events reported on page 1, column 2 of the *New York Times* influence ones described on page 5, column 1. In my language: Kite flying does not usually bring with it a power goal-directed towards lifting doors. Nor does it do so in this case. In this case, it brings with it the power of the *double pulley*: pulling up on the input end of a double-pulley rope influences the force experienced by objects tied on the output end. It does so not on account of

---

[78] To see this pencil sharpener, look in Cartwright and Hardie 2012, 77.

being a kite flying but because, in the arrangements of the Rube Goldberg machine, the kite flying is pulling on the input end of a double-pulley rope.

This is the kind of point I have made before about the relation of the abstract to the concrete. The concrete is what the abstract amounts to in the case at hand.[79] What is new here is the recognition of the central importance of the arrangements.[80] The abstract/concrete distinction is not the same as that between determinable and determinate, and I can now offer one good indication of this. Being scarlet is—and is always—a way of being red. But being a kite-flying is not usually a way of being a pulling on the input end of a double-pulley rope. It is so in this arrangement but not in most others. So, arrangements matter. They fix what policy variables can do.

2. iii The Concatenation Problem

Look at the second step of the pencil-sharpening process. Pulling up a little door does not normally free moths. It does so because, in this arrangement, the pulling up of the door is the breaching of a closed container and this has the power to allow mobile contents to escape. If we stay at the abstract level, we have a problem. At stage 1, an upward force on the input end of a double-pulley rope raises a weight at the output end.[81] We can represent that thus:

$$U \rightarrow R$$

At stage 2, breaching a closed container allows mobile contents to escape, which we can represent thus:

$$B \rightarrow E$$

These do not concatenate. How then does the initial activity of kite flying participate in producing the outcome of the moths eating the flannel, let alone the final sharpening of pencils?

---

[79] Cartwright 1999.

[80] This has been brought home to me by working with John Pemberton. It is also a central pillar of many hylomorphic accounts of powers.

[81] I have oversimplified here to make the point clear. Even staying just with the diagram, let alone moving to the embodied machine, other factors play a role at every stage; for instance, both gravity and friction influence the raising of the door in addition to the upward pulling from the pulley rope. But these omissions do not matter for the point at hand.

The answer again lies in the arrangement. R and B are different features. But, due to the arrangement, they are concretely instantiated in the very same happening: the opening of the little door. In this arrangement, the raising of a weight at the output end of a double pulley (R) *is* the opening of the door (d) and the opening of the door (d) *is* the breaching of a closed container (B). That's how kite-flying (k) leads to the moths' being free to eat the flannel (m):

$$U = k, U \rightarrow R, R = d, d = B, B \rightarrow E, E = m$$
$$\text{Therefore: } k \rightarrow d \rightarrow m.$$

3. Context Matters

The lesson of the first problem is that policy variables generally don't have the power to influence the policy outcomes we want them for. We can label *mass* as geared for influencing the force experienced by other masses and *charge* as geared for influencing the force experienced by other charges. But we cannot label *deworming* as geared for raising reading ability or *breeding in captivity* as geared for increasing the number of functioning adults, neither for raptors, for which *Conservation Evidence* says it is "likely to be beneficial,"[82] nor for foxes, where we know there was success on Santa Cruz Island. Typical policy variables can't get us very far.

The lesson from the last two problems is that arrangements are crucial to what outputs can be produced from what inputs. The slogan for this in evidence-based policy is 'context matters'. This is widely recognized. What happens once policies are initiated differs from place to place. Nevertheless, the intervention-centered approach strongly dominates the scene and it does not pay serious attention to context. As just one example, consider what Hakan Seckinelgin reports from one of the huge Biannual International AIDS conferences (Seckinelgin works on international HIV-AIDS policies in sub-Saharan Africa):

> [T]he then executive director of [the] International AIDS Society (IAS) . . . emphasized the importance [of] the social sciences and their contributions . . . [H]e highlighted . . . the way in which social sciences can still help to think about behaviour and the context of behaviour change as well as to provide pathways for dealing with the consequences of changes in the international aid regime.

---
[82] Dicks et al. 2017.

After this positive, but generic statement, he ... argue[d] that in the end *HIV is a medical condition and that we expect the advances in this area will have the biggest impact on the disease* ... Given [this], the social sciences, the audience was told, will have to make sure that their added value is clear ...[83]

Seckinelgin also tells us that at these meetings researchers and policy experts give excited talks about the effectiveness of a newly tested treatment or preventive strategy. Generally it is only in the very last sentence that they add 'But of course context matters'.

As a concrete example, consider an HIV-AIDS policy currently being considered for wide adoption across sub-Saharan Africa.[84] PREP (Pre-exposure prophylaxis) is a pill used to stop transmission of HIV from HIV positive to HIV negative individuals, particularly men-who-have-sex-with-men (MSM). The main trials showing effectiveness were carried out in the US and France. Subsequently, policy intervention programs to make PREP widely available to MSM have been implemented in several Western contexts, such as San Francisco and Paris. In these contexts, signs are that it has been successful in significantly reducing HIV infection rates among MSM. It is often described as 'a powerful addition to the arsenal of weapons' to address HIV.[85]

UNAIDS has been promoting PREP interventions in African countries to reduce HIV infection rates there. The underlying assumption is that if PREP works in Western contexts, it should work in Africa, and implementing it there is the right thing to do. Kenya already has a PREP program, and both Botswana and Zimbabwe are developing guidelines. Let's think about Kenya. There are significant structural differences between the Kenyan context and Western contexts, like San Francisco and Paris, that may have important implications for whether the policy is likely to work there. In particular, unlike in the US or in France, in Kenya:

- Homosexual acts are illegal[86]
- It is culturally unacceptable to admit openly to MSM acts or to self-identify as a sexual group that engages in MSM acts

---

[83] Seckinelgin 2017, 8.

[84] For more on these kinds of concerns and the surrounding research see Seckinelgin 2017; Seckinelgin and Paternotte 2015. See also, UNAIDS 2016. On effectiveness of PREP in different populations, see NAM Publications 2018.

[85] See, for example, Jones 2014.

[86] There is this anomaly in Kenya: same sex activity is criminalized but their HIV plans, e.g. for trials, explicitly include MSM populations. This is because of pressure from international actors and international policy priorities.

- The categories which defined the populations in Western studies—gay men having unsafe sex, drug users, transgender people, sex workers—are not categories in which Kenyans tend to self-identify
- These are not even concepts in terms of which many Kenyans think
- It would be difficult to have anonymous access to the treatment, especially in the countryside, even if available over the counter
- If the Kenyan government were explicitly to target the MSM group, this privileging for resource allocation of a group that engages in illegal acts would likely be politically contentious, given the local culture and norms, and so difficult to sustain politically.

This has a couple of implications. First, if a policy in Kenya were to be targeted at MSM groups, it seems unlikely that those groups would come forward, because it is illegal, culturally unacceptable, and they don't think of themselves under these descriptions. Accepting the treatment makes one's culturally unacceptable sexual practices public. Second, the Kenyan government would be unlikely to target the intervention explicitly to MSM as this would conflict with existing laws. In this case, policy might be targeted to a wider population, which includes MSM but in which MSM are not explicitly identified as such, perhaps the adult population more generally. But effectiveness amongst this wider group is not as warranted from the trials and this would lead to wider medication/side-effects.

To connect back to the main discussion, recall Millikan's oil drop experiment. In Millikan's arrangement pictured in Figure 1.3, the positive charges at the top plate attract the negative charges on the drop, and all the powers acting together bring the drop to a standstill. Towfic Shomar has constructed a very different arrangement in which one negative charge repels another but that moves the two closer together.[87] The lesson is that what effect can be achieved when a cause exercises depends on what other powers exercise and on the arrangements in which they do so. Similarly, the arrangements in which a program to offer PREP would operate in Kenya, and especially outside Nairobi, are substantially different from those in Paris. Villages do not offer the anonymity of big cities, the laws are different, the cultural norms are different, and the terms in which people think are different.

---

[87] I also mentioned this apparatus in footnote 7, Lecture 2.

4. What Is the Intervention-centered Approach Good For?

The intervention-centered approach, recall, focuses on intervention/outcome pairs. The bulk of the efforts in What Works Centers go into vetting and synthesizing studies that test whether the intervention 'causes' the targeted outcome in studied populations, for instance, in Figure 3.1 we see that *Conservation Evidence* reviewed five studies looking at whether breeding raptors in captivity improved or increased adult populations in the sites where it was implemented.[88] We philosophers spend a lot of time considering what the relation 'causes' consists in. That is not my concern here. Let us at least agree with J. L. Mackie that the relation is asymmetric and irreflexive and that causes are INUS conditions for their effects[89]

$$E\ c= C_1A_1 + \ldots + C_nA_n$$

Where *c*= marks the asymmetric singular 'causes' relation, the *C*s designate salient causal factors for E and the *A*s, a (possibly long) conjunction of other factors that are necessary along with C to produce E. Jeremy Hardie and I[90] call the factors represented by the *A*s, 'support factors'; they are also called 'moderator' or 'interactive' variables. The standard philosophical example, recall from Lecture 2, is oxygen: Striking a match (C) can cause a flame (E), but only if oxygen is there as well (A).

Where variables are non-dichotomous, we have by analogy a *generalized Mackie formula*:[91]

$$\text{GMF: In } \varphi, \forall i[Y(i)\ c= \alpha(i)X(i) + W(i)].$$

Because my focus is on the single factor represented by X (say, 'breeding raptors in captivity'), I have gathered all the additive factors into W. I have also added an explicit reference to the population, φ, in which the formula is supposed to hold for every individual i. This population relativization is important for policy deliberation—none of the formulae involving real social and economic policies are like '**F** = m**a**', expected to hold everywhere;

---

[88] Sutherland et al. 2015.
[89] Mackie 1965. An INUS condition is an insufficient but necessary part of an unnecessary but sufficient condition. Note that the claim that causes are INUS conditions does not imply that INUS conditions are causes
[90] Hardie and Cartwright 2012.
[91] Also called a *potential outcomes equation*.

yet the populations are often not specified in practice, which encourages sloppy inferences that contribute to ineffective policies. I have also added the universal quantifier since that is what is implied by the use of these formulae in EBP. I'll call propositions of GMF form, *Mackie claims*.

Mackie claims are at the heart of the intervention-centered approach, where they are taken

- to record a set of causes sufficient to fix the value (or probability)[92] of Y for each individual i in φ
- to imply counterfactuals about the of value Y given various settings of right-hand-side variables for individuals in φ.

Consider, for example, the randomized controlled trial (RCT), which is supposed to be the gold standard for establishing 'What Works'. We would like to know a counterfactual value: the *individual treatment effect* for each individual in the population, i.e. how much difference having the intervention (X = 1) versus not having it (X = 0) would make to that individual. Clearly this cannot be observed. The wonderful thing about RCTs is that they provide an estimate of the *average individual treatment effect* across the population enrolled in the RCT even though we can't observe the values to be averaged. It is easy to show that, for an ideal RCT,[93] the observed difference in average outcome values between the treatment and control groups is an unbiased estimate of the average individual treatment effect in the RCT population, *Exp α*.[94]

$$Exp\ (O/T) - Exp\ (O/\text{-}T) = Exp\ α\ in\ φ$$

Return now to the intervention-centered approach, which hopes to use evidence about how an intervention has influenced the targeted outcome in some population φ, or small set of populations, in aid of predicting policy outcomes in new populations.[95] So, in what new populations can an inter-

---

[92] Where probabilities are involved, this is generally represented by adding an 'error' term into W (and possibly α) for which a probability distribution is supposed.

[93] 'Ideal' means that the orthogonality conditions (X probabilistically independent of α,W) are satisfied, which is what we aim for with random assignment, blinding, and post assignment policing for sources of confounding.

[94] Note that the fact that the observed difference is an unbiased estimate of the average treatment effect does not imply that the observed outcome is anywhere close to the true average. For more on 'Understanding and Misunderstanding Randomized Controlled Trials' see the joint paper of that title by Angus Deaton and me (2017).

vention contribute in the same way as in the study population φ? This is exactly analogous to the question of where else besides my study flying a kite will affect the sharpening of pencils. If my arguments in these lectures are correct, the answer is:

> The same connection can hold between intervention and outcome in a new population as in φ if the powers and arrangements that allow this connection are sufficiently alike in the two populations.

This catapults us into the domain of the context-centered approach. We need to understand the details of the local arrangements. That is extremely difficult. We have no standard methodology for what the relevant facts are and were we to be in possession of them, it is very difficult to figure out what causal laws they will afford and what not. Sometimes we are lucky though and can revert to the intervention-centered approach. I turn to that next.

5. Voodoo: When the Intervention-centered Approach Works

To see when we can expect the intervention-centered approach to work, I detour through some work of Michael Strevens. Just as I have long argued,[96] Strevens supposes that a great many of our scientific laws, when rendered as proper claims, hold only ceteris paribus (*cp*), and that one of the central references in the ceteris paribus condition needed to render these true (or true enough, etc.) must be to the mechanism that gives rise to them[97]—what I have called a *nomological machine*. A nomological machine is constituted by features with powers exercising together in stable (enough) arrangements, where, as I have been arguing here, we should take these to be Trias powers, and we need to be especially heedful of the arrangements—e.g., that the kite string is threaded under and over two pulley wheels or that bald eagles are nesting in the trees around the island.

---

[95] Though there is increasing concern to find ways to learn *for whom* in the population the treatment is likely to work and *for whom* not. Note that for the same average treatment effect to obtain in two populations, we need not only that the same GMF holds, as I discuss here, but also that the support factors have the same average. What having the same GMF guarantees is that at least the intervention can help in the new population if only the support factors are right.
[96] Cartwright 1989.
[97] Strevens 2012.

Strevens renders

'Ceteris paribus, in conditions Z, Fs cause Gs'

as

'By way of the target mechanism M, the conditions Z and the property F bring about the property G.'[98]

Strevens says, "When a causal hypothesis is framed it is supposed to make a claim about a particular contextually determined mechanism: the target mechanism."[99] He supposes that the context and practices with respect to cp laws of the kind he addresses are sufficient to secure reference to the intended mechanism among interested parties.[100]

He titles his paper 'Voodoo that works' because the facts about M that make the cp causal regularity claim true "are typically opaque to the scientists who formulate and test them."[101] This is because, although these scientists can refer to the mechanism that they have in mind, they often cannot describe the details of what it consists in, how it is put together, nor how it gives rise to the causal regularity. This, he says, is what a good scientific model that explains the cp regularity will do.

This power of ceteris paribus hedges may seem to be not only miraculous but useless. What is the practical significance of content in a hypothesis unless the investigators know that it is there? My collaborators, Sarah Wieten and John Pemberton, and I think this is where the real voodoo lies.[102] The reference to mechanisms is opaque but we can still put our cp claims to good use. That we can do so is key to much of daily and scientific life. It is also

---

[98] This is his first rendering. He later offers a more refined reading that adds something akin to my NE (nothing-else relevant obtains) clause. Since this is not directly relevant to my points right here, I will talk in terms of the simpler version.

[99] By contrast with what Sarah Wieten and I call *empty* accounts, ones that do not fill in the clause so that the cp law does not even make a functioning claim; by contrast, on Strevens's account, cp laws have content. In any concrete cp claim, M is filled in (if only implicitly) by a term that refers to a specific mechanism. It also contrasts with *boring* accounts, ones that simply assert that *there are* some conditions under which the cp causal regularity holds, which will often turn out to be trivially true.

[100] This does then require a theory of reference that permits this, which Strevens does not discuss. But this does not seem an unreasonable demand on a theory of reference and I won't discuss it either.

[101] Strevens 2012, 652.

[102] Cartwright, Wieten, and Pemberton 2018.

key to successful use of the intervention-centered approach. But successes depend on the availability of sufficient *markers* and *cautions*.

- *Markers.* In many cases there are recognizable markers for when the right arrangements are likely to obtain and when not. Often these are ones we can come to learn and learn without understanding what the arrangements are. (Toasters come with labels; acorns have a recognizable look to them . . .)
- *Cautions.* We also come to learn some of the ways in which our interventions must be and must not be carried out if we are to avoid disturbing the arrangements that afford the intervention-outcome process. (Don't plant red acorns till the spring; don't drop the toaster into the dishwasher . . .)

So, when does the voodoo of the intervention-centered approach work? An intervention-centered approach is likely to produce reasonably reliable predictions about a policy/outcome pair for a given collection of different populations if it uses reliable markers for picking populations in which to implement the policy and enough reliable cautions about how to implement it. We are justified in expecting its predictions to be reliable if we have good warrant that the markers and cautions used are reliable. That seems a tall order. But it is not at all out of the question that in many cases there is enough expertise available to fill it. Even casual knowledge can get us started.

Consider the fictional example used by Nobel-prize-winning economist Angus Deaton[103] in discussing limitations on the usefulness of knowledge that comes from RCTs and in criticizing the bases for many of the recommendations in Abhijit Banerjee and Esther Duflo's influential book, *Poor Economics: A Radical Rethinking of the Way to Fight Global Poverty*. Deaton considers two schools, St Joseph's and St Mary's. St Mary's is thinking of adopting a new training program for which there have been very well conducted RCTs in some schools somewhere else. A meta-analyisis pooling results says that, on average, the training program improved test scores by some given amount across these schools. St Joseph's, just down the road, adopted this program and got a significantly different outcome. What should St Mary's do? Deaton notes that St Mary's is not the mean, and it may be a long way from it. (Recall that an RCT estimates the *average* treatment effect in the study populations). He argues "The mean is useful, and will be considered, but it is not decisive. St Joe's may be closer, more 'like' St

---

[103] Deaton 2012. Also in Deaton and Cartwright 2017.

Mary's, and may have got similar results in the past, [b]etter than an average over unlike schools."[104] Here Deaton relies on a loose common-sense evaluation of what kinds of things matter—what I have called 'markers'. Deaton concludes that it is "[n]ot obvious, or clear that St Joe is not a better guide than the RCT, or indeed an anecdote about another school." (His overall recommendation, however, leans to the context-centered approach: "Perhaps the board of St Mary's could go to St Joe's and see the new policy in action . . .").[105]

For a second example, consider the PREP intervention again. Until I started to look into it with Seckinelgin, I didn't know anything about either legal or cultural norms in Kenya, nor about sexual practices there, nor about the concepts Kenyans use to think about themselves or these practices. But, from listening to the Sunday morning news in the UK, I knew that Kenya is heavily Christian—almost 85%—and of that, a good chunk is in the Anglican Church of Kenya, which in 2014 put a five-year moratorium on the appointment of women bishops. I also know that there's been a good deal of US evangelical activism in East Africa. These are not well-evidenced markers but they are red flags about presuming that the arrangements in Kenya will support a reasonably smooth process from the introduction of a PREP program to a reduction in HIV infections.

The trick in all cases of course is to be able to give reasons in defense of claims about markers and cautions, to judge how much we can trust to them, and to hedge our bets accordingly. There is one popular kind of inference in this regard I want to warn against: using the selection criteria for trial populations as markers. By themselves these tell us virtually nothing about where else an intervention will work, though of course we may have *independent* reason for thinking they are relevant. Let me explain.

Researchers conducting RCTs are urged to be explicit in reporting their results about the inclusion and exclusion criteria for participating in their study. This is supposed to be in aid of judging the wider applicability of the study results. For instance, from the *British Medical Journal*: "Many users of trial information rely on published journal articles. These articles generally do not reflect the exact definition of the study population as prespecified in the protocol. Incomplete or inadequate reporting of eligibility criteria hampers a proper assessment of the applicability of trial results."[106] This is

---

[104] Deaton 2012.
[105] Deaton 2012.
[106] Blümle et al. 2011.

a mistake. Trial population selection criteria give little clue to applicability. Suppose you know that all the individuals in a study satisfied description D. Maybe they were all free of renal and bone disease and within the San Francisco Public Health System, as in one of the PREP trials I mentioned.[107] What can you learn from that?

There are three roles you might see this information playing.

First, it could be information relevant internally to a Mackie claim. We know that the average treatment effect for Y of an intervention X in a population of individuals described by the same Mackie claim depends on the expectation, Exp (α), of the net effect of the support factors[108] for X with respect to Y in that population. Suppose we are, unusually, in an excellent epistemic situation: We know that D implies that every member of that population has the same value for α. Then we can draw strong conclusions. The observed average is not just an unbiased estimate of the true average for the study population, it is the true average and the true average is the actual value for everyone in the study population. Sadly, this has no bearing on our original problem of wider applicability. We know that the results can hold wherever the same Mackie claim holds. But the study results, even coupled with the knowledge that we have studied a population totally homogenous with respect to the support factors for X to influence Y there, tells us nothing about which other populations satisfy the same Mackie claim. In particular, the support factors for the study population may be totally irrelevant in the target population and there may be no support factors in the target that would allow it to influence the outcome there.[109]

Second, imagine that we still take the information to be relevant internally to a Mackie claim but D includes factors not in α and excludes some that are. What can we conclude? Almost nothing. We can still get an unbiased estimate of the average treatment effect for that population. But we cannot conclude much about D even for target populations where the same Mackie claim holds. If D includes factors not in α and omits others, then, as always, if the *true* average treatment effect (ATE) > 0, this implies that at least someone in the study population with D was helped, so someone satisfying D was helped. So: (*True* ATE > 0 in φ) and (φ and ψ satisfy the same Mackie claim) → D does not *ensure* the treatment is *in*effective in ψ.

---

[107] San Francisco Health Network 2016.

[108] Recall, also called 'moderator' or 'interactive' variables.

[109] This is important for other reasons, so my criticisms do not imply that it is okay to be sloppy about this.

Which is not all that much to learn, and that is supposing we can help ourselves to the assumption that the arrangements in φ and ψ are sufficiently similar to support the same input-output relations between intervention and outcome (reflected in satisfying the same Mackie claim). Any further conclusions depend *entirely* on other information. This is bad news for the intervention-centered approach.

The medical literature sometimes hopes to overcome some of this problem with *pragmatic trials*. Here is a typical claim from the *British Medical Journal*: "The pragmatic attitude favours design choices that *maximise applicability of the trial's results to usual care settings*, rely on unarguably important outcomes such as mortality and severe morbidity, and are tested in a wide range of participants."[110] To this end pragmatic trials tend to have looser eligibility conditions, for instance with respect to co-morbidities and other drugs, and be set in more realistic circumstances, for instance with 'ordinary' clinicians and 'ordinary' patients. But the bad news is still the same. RCTs—any RCTs[111]—show results about the trial population only, and even for other populations similar enough to satisfy the same Mackie claim, unless you know that the inclusion and exclusion criteria, D, pick out a population with the same value for (the net effect of) the support factors (or the same distribution over these), you don't learn what you'd hoped. You might think you can conclude, e.g. 'At least it doesn't matter to have less expert clinicians.' But you can't: Less expert clinicians might be offset by some positive feature in the pragmatic trial setting.

Third, the inclusion and exclusion criteria might serve as markers for populations that are sufficiently similar so that they satisfy the same Mackie claim and hence could have the same average treatment effect.[112] That's when they can be really helpful for generalization. Probably this is the way to see pragmatic trials. We may not know much of the details of what the generally healthy young men are like who get enrolled in a normal trial but we know enough to bet that they are sufficiently different from elderly people with a number of illnesses and taking a number of different drugs

---

[110] Zwarenstein et al. 2008 (my emphasis).

[111] Indeed, any study. Studies can only establish facts about the systems studied. To extrapolate to other systems, we need additional assumptions from elsewhere. (This is key to my 'argument theory of evidence' (Cartwright 2013a) and John Norton's 'material theory of induction' mentioned in Lecture 1.)

[112] Depending of course on the distribution of support factors, which are represented by α. Even with the same Mackie claim true, average treatment effects can even be different in sign if balance of positive-contributing and negative-contributing support factors differs.

to predict that the social, psychological, and physiological arrangements in the elderly will not support the same intervention-outcome relations that obtain for the young men. This kind of negative conclusion can be helpful of course. It makes us more cautious about expecting the same results elsewhere. But what we really need are reliable positive markers, and these seem harder to come by and harder to justify.

6. THE CONTEXT-CENTERED APPROACH

Both the intervention-centered and the context-centered approach want to use accumulated knowledge to improve predictions about policy effectiveness in a target population. This is a laudable aim we can all endorse. We are not likely to make reliable predictions about policy outcomes about new cases without relying on past knowledge. The problem with intervention-centering is that it is too limited in the range of knowledge it employs. It looks chiefly at whether the policy has worked elsewhere; then it uses loosely warranted markers to settle whether the new site is sufficiently similar to those where the policy has been successful to support the same causal pathways. The context-centered approach takes on the difficult job that intervention-centering ducks: understanding the details of the new context well enough to figure out what causal pathways it can and cannot afford. Context centering can have real advantages. It should not only provide more reliable predictions about the effectiveness of the proposed policy in the new site; it can also ground new proposals for bespoke policies geared to the causal pathways available there. That is, it will have these advantages if we can do it successfully. Which is a big if. This is why I am on a campaign to develop ways to do it better. One thing I know for certain: to figure out what process of change a new situation can support will require a vast amount knowledge of very different varieties as well as a great deal of know-how.

Return to the start of these lectures for an example. Suppose you are given the job of post hoc evaluation of Millikan's apparatus, pictured in Figure 1.3, and his proposed procedures. You are to judge whether or not they support the theory of change that is supposed to produce an accurate measurement of the charge on a drop. We can, with much oversimplification, take the theory of change to be something like this: An oil drop is sprayed into the chamber; it starts to fall; the chamber is ionized; electrons attach themselves to the drop; the light source illuminates the drops so they look like bright stars as they move; the stars are watched through a viewing microscope; the knob controlling the voltage is turned till the drop is observed to come to rest; the potential difference (PD) between the plates (and thus the excess positive charge on the top plate) is measured accurately; the drag of the air is calculated from Stokes's principle using pre-measured values of α, μ, v, A, and l; the pull of gravity is calculated using measured values for the mass of the drop; the Coulomb force, and thus the charge on the drop, is calculated supposing the only factors affecting the drop's motion are the pull of gravity and the drag of the air.

What will you have to do to reach a sound verdict? Here the two models of the Millikan experiment—Figure 1.1 and Figure 1.2—give the key. You will want to be able to establish that the apparatus and procedures match the models:

> MAM (Model-Apparatus Match): The apparatus (pictured in Figure 1.3) embodies all the features depicted in the two models and nothing else at any stage that could significantly influence what is supposed to happen under the theory of change at the next stage.

To estimate the goodness of fit of the apparatus to the model, you will want to learn all the things I mentioned in Lecture 1. These include a number of principles in physics, some known by us all, like Gravity, Coulomb's principle, and vector addition, some less well known, like the adjusted Stokes's principle and the long list of features that restrict its applicability; you must be sure that there will be no significant influences on the drop's motions except the total force calculated from these three sources; you must know that Millikan used clock oil and know that the viscosity of clock oil is little affected by temperature change (otherwise the viscosity measurements cannot be trusted) and that clock oil has a low tendency to spread or evaporate (so the drop lived long enough to catch electrons and so that it retained its spherical shape so that the adjusted Stokes's principle could apply); that the ionization procedure creates electrons in the chamber and that these can and do attach themselves to the drop; that the viewing microscope allows accurate enough observation; etc.; etc.

To get a concrete grasp of the problems the evaluator faces it is helpful think of this knowledge under two headings: knowledge of the positives and knowledge of the negatives. Positive: for accurate potential difference (PD) readings, it is a good idea to use a 900-volt Kelvin and White electrostatic voltmeter (as Millikan did). Negative: nothing in the apparatus or procedures should get in the way of the voltmeter taking an accurate reading. The first is a rule of thumb; it may be 'on the books' already or it may take serious work to figure out. Recall the Gravity Probe gyroscopes I mentioned at the start of Lecture 1. These needed to be perfectly spherical and perfectly homogenous. After years of research and development, the Gravity Probe B team figured that a 1.5-inch sphere of fused quartz, polished and lapped to within a few atomic layers would fit the bill, and they were able to produce some of these spheres.[113] As to the negatives, there is seldom a fixed list to go by. There may be some common things to watch out for. But there's always something more that can go wrong. This is familiar in ordinary life from the difficulties of writing effective regulation. We either leave things at an abstract level—insurance sellers have a duty of care to their customers—which doesn't tell us what this consists in on the ground; or, we write a long list of specifics. But there's almost always ways to satisfy all the requirements in that long list and still to bilk your customers. This is why I say it takes know-how. It cannot be done by the book; it takes art.

That's the sticking point in the evidence-based policy movement. They don't like art. They don't trust *techné*; they want *episteme*; and above all they want a book, a book that allows the 'objective' policing of claims so that the claims are not open to whim, political maneuvering, or conscious or unconscious bias. If I am right, what they want is impossible when it comes to modeling real embodied situations. Everyone agrees that it is at least difficult. That is the appeal of the intervention-centered approach. We don't model. We look for markers that the situation—that we wouldn't know how to model—is right, hopefully reliable markers that have 'objective' warrant.

But you never get anything for free in this domain. As I noted, reliable markers are hard to come by; small differences can matter. For example, in one setting girls as well as boys are sent to school as a result of a scheme incentivizing parents for attendance, but in another, similar-seeming setting the girls refuse to go because "their latrines are next to those of the boys, who taunt and humiliate them."[114] Equally important, we have no good, agreed-upon methodology for warranting when proposed features are markers. I don't think we even have any good rules of thumb, agreed upon or not. Without these, we must rely on techné—which may not be

---

[113] This is why I used the left-hand side and the right-hand side of a block of fused quartz in Lecture 2 as an example of genuine 'component-hood' where all the parts are just the same kind of thing as the whole they make up.

[114] Woolcock 2016.

too bad if we can find experts with lots of know-how; otherwise it looks like pure whim, or worse. Unfortunately, neither alternative lives up to the demands of evidence-based policy.

7. In Sum

Both the intervention-centered and the context-centered approach need know-how; neither can be done by the book. Both are inevitably open to political manipulation, bias, and straightforward mistake. Neither will be able to produce predictions we can be highly certain of. These are facts of life. There's no good supposing these problems would go away if only we did it better. We surely can do it better, especially if we devote effort to learning how to manage the problems and not just to getting more and more nuggets of knowledge to write in our books.

I began these lectures with metaphysics and I have ended with practice. That's because the metaphysics matters to what practices can work, and how. I've praised engineers and cooks and inventors, as well as experimental physicists like Millikan and Melissa Franklin, who helped gather the first evidence for the top quark; my UK neighbor, John O'Connor, who designed the Oxford knee; the team who evacuated Fort McMurray; those who worked on wartime radar—like Lee Davenport (who developed the Signal Corps Radio radar that helped counter the German air force and whom I have a soft spot for since he and I both got our Bachelor of Science degrees from the University of Pittsburgh); and the Stanford Gravity Probe team. I have praised these for being artful modelers. We need artful modeling. We cannot make reliable predictions without it. And I have personified Nature, which I'm sure many have found objectionable. That is to underline the lesson that we cannot do away with techné by writing bigger and bigger books. We must be artful modelers because Nature herself is an artful modeler.

Afterword: Nature, the Artful Bartender

Richard Vagnino

[When we discussed these lectures in the UCSD Philosophy of Science graduate seminar in January 2019, Andrew Bollhagen suggested that Nature employs archetypes not rules, and Richard Vagnino compared Nature, the Artful Modeler of empirical events to Nature, the Artful Bartender. Here is his account.—NC]

Nature, the Artful Bartender, makes the best drinks in town. Motivated by a desire to understand how she can craft so many incredible cocktails without sacrificing speed or consistency, you pull up a seat at the bar to observe. You study her movements carefully—the bottles she selects, the quantities she pours—and after some time, you become convinced that you have discovered a few general principles that govern how much of each ingredient to use per cocktail. You believe, for instance, that when Nature shakes a cocktail, she uses two ounces of the hard stuff, followed by one ounce of sweet and one ounce of sour. Confident that you have cracked the code, you begin to shake up a few cocktails of your own, following what you take to be the recipe that Nature is following; however, it quickly becomes clear that this principle is far too crude for the purpose at hand. Your drinks, compared to Nature's, seem clumsy, unbalanced, and surprisingly inconsistent.

Undaunted, you turn your attention back to Nature, and informed by your recent libationary shortcomings, you notice that Nature seems to adjust the recipe depending on the spirit. Accordingly, you begin to alter your proportions of sugar and citrus for bourbon versus gin, for rum versus vodka. The results are more promising than your initial attempts, but the gulf between what you observe in Nature and your own concoctions remains dispiritingly large. So, with an eye to Nature, you continue to tinker and make minor adjustments. You realize that not only does the spirit matter, but the producer, and not only the producer but the batch, even the individual bottle. You see Nature compensating for minor variances in volume: an extra sixteenth of an ounce of one ingredient offset by a minor adjustment to its compliment. You begin to notice differences in the juices you use—their variable ripeness, the time since they were squeezed—and assume Nature must adjust accordingly as well. You begin to add additional ingredients, liqueurs and digestifs—oddly shaped bottles that Nature occasionally pulled off the shelf suddenly begin to take on new meaning as your capacity to control and predict flavor, viscosity, acidity, and heat grow exponentially. Other bits of knowledge are even harder to explain. You notice, and quickly learn to emulate, the different ways that Nature shakes the tin depending on the size and quality of the ice, as well as the constitution of the beverage. You start to appreciate the subtle ways in which the oil of a lemon peel or the refreshing quality of a mint sprig can alter the entire experience of the drink.

As you proceed, you are struck by the unmistakable impression that to deliver the sort of precision and quality you've come to expect from her, Nature, the Artful Bartender, must be expertly keeping track of all of these details as well. By the end of this process you realize, you can furnish a highly detailed model of an individual drink—the exact volumes of the ingredients, adjusted to account for any number of eccentricities in the ingredients (e.g. discrepancies between the sweetness of syrups); the number, quality, and shape of ice cubes; the exact amount of time the drink was shaken and how (e.g. 2-step, 3-step, or butterfly Japanese hard-shake); which glassware was used, how was it chilled and for how long—but no set of general principles or inviolable laws that will safely guide you from start to finish. Rather, to create cocktails as Nature creates them, you must artfully deploy a vast and often heterogeneous suite of skills and knowledge flexibly, taking into account a constant stream of unpredictable and seemingly indefinite factors. What's more, having reached this conclusion through the slow, deliberative process of observation and imitation (not to mention a generous dash of guided trial and error), you suspect that Nature must cope with these same challenges the same way you do; that is, Nature is an Artful Bartender.

PART 2

Further Thoughts on Contingency and Order

4

Is the Cat Really Lapping Up the Milk?

Introduction

This paper is about a dispute, or at least a difference, between Bas van Fraassen and me about possibility. There are possibilities in nature, I maintain, not just in the model, as van Fraassen would have it. They depend, I maintain, on facts that hold in our world—the only world there is—and not on what is supposed to happen in other worlds that I can't see existing but that David Lewis latterly endorsed, nor on laws of nature, writ I don't know where. So they at least do not deploy these two techniques that neither van Fraassen nor I hold with.

There are possibilities in nature because the future is open but constrained, or so I claim any account would have it that is based, as Otto Neurath described, in the 'earthly plane' and not in some hidden and secret world above, behind, or in a better place than here. The methodology that supports this is a kind of 'commonsense' empiricism, that the world is pretty much as we observe it to be until we have very good reason to the contrary, following the sentiments of Willard Duncan Vandiver: "I come from a state that raises corn and cotton and cockleburs and Democrats, and frothy eloquence neither convinces nor satisfies me. I am from Missouri. You have got to show me."[115]

Thick Causal Relations and Their Place in the World

Besides possibilia, there is another kind of fact that makes up the commonsense world I think I live in that van Fraassen also seems to deny: facts about

---

[115] As quoted in *The State of Missouri: An Introduction*.

'causal relations' or 'causal processes'. I begin with the causal relations. Note the *s*. I do not maintain that we see in nature any such thing as *the causal relation*—the kind of thing that Hume looked for and could not find in his experience. I can't find it in mine either. Rather we see thousands of relations that for different purposes on different occasions we label 'causal', a view I share with my colleague Julian Reiss. As I noted in chapter 2 and will visit again in chapter 5, the world where I live is full of pushings, pullings, nourishings, lapping ups, openings, closings, attractings, repellings; Reiss adds a number of 'causatives' that he sees at play in different scientific and everyday settings: feed, kill, secrete, transduce, gouge, upset.

Recent philosophy of science has tended to take the causal relation to be sui generis, not reducible to any noncausal relations; and has put much effort into finding some central characterizing features of it. No offering though has been much agreed on and all seem to have counterexamples. Van Fraassen, like Peter Menzies and others, turns to agency. All these have their roots in our conception that we are agents, persons, who do things: 'it is from talk of agency that all other causal talk is derivative'. I too have long connected causality with what we can do. My first paper, defending that there are causes in nature, is titled "Causal Laws and Effective Strategies" (1979): Spraying swamps with bacterial larvicide is not merely correlated with the disappearance of mosquitoes; it is an effective way to get rid of them. But it is not merely a matter of what *we* do—'spraying bacterial larvicide', agency that we metaphorically extend to the larvicide; it is a matter of what the larvicide itself does—it eventually starves the mosquito larvae, hence warranting our claim that it causes the mosquitoes to disappear.

This is just upside down from what van Fraassen endorses:

> "[The dishwasher] is washing the dishes".... that is a metaphorical extension of the concept of dish washing—it is us who are really washing the dishes mechanically, with this machine, rather than manually, that is all. It is easy to get befuddled about this, because technological progress reduces the human element, the agency involved on our part, to a more and more practically negligible amount—but that makes no difference of principle.
>
> *The dishwashing machine washes dishes only in the sense that a typewriter types.*

All those nomological machines that leave the laboratory to perform so splendidly in our service become, in common parlance, *animate*: they do and act and use and even calculate, control, adjust, and drive, in our descriptions of what happens when they are set in motion. That form of discourse is our currently harmless form of pagan animism. Harmless; but let's not let it dictate our philosophy.[116]

Beware though. The claim that not just us but the causes themselves bring about outcomes does not mean that these causal activities consist of two kinds of features: a set of purely 'non-modal' ones—features that van Fraassen and contemporary 'Humeans' would allow to be both in the representation and in the world—and then a 'causal' relation that for them holds only in the model but for others may hold in the world as well, perhaps the kind of necessitation relation that Hume looked for. Sprayings, smotherings, pushings, pullings, and the like are rather *thick* causal relations, on the model of Bernard Williams's thick normative features, like 'sleazy', 'heroic', 'mean', 'welcoming'. Williams explains that the corresponding concepts are both 'world guided' and 'action guiding', but they do not divide into a non-normative 'descriptive' component with a normative judgment, like 'good' or 'bad', added on, which is to be made sense of by a higher moral theory, like utilitarianism, Kantianism, or some religious doctrine. Williams claims that we can make true claims using these concepts—so long as we don't attribute this two-part composition to them. That's because there are no acceptable moral theories to characterize just what the good and the bad amount to.[117]

The same I claim is true of our thick causal concepts. They are not a combination of a descriptive component with necessitation added on since there is no acceptable theory to characterize what necessitation consists in. As with Williams's thick moral concepts, these thick causal concepts face two directions—they are simultaneously *evidence-guided* and *prediction-guiding*. The concepts are evidence guided in that we look to the facts that currently obtain to police their application, and they are prediction guiding since we can use them to help figure out what facts will obtain.

As van Fraassen and I agree, these concepts are in the model, as I insist they must be if the model is to be empirically adequate (whether empirical adequacy demands getting right what is available to us through our senses or, as I would have it, getting right the concrete facts of the world we live in). That's because they are, equally, in the world that is modeled. There is nothing ephemeral about their referents that means they cannot live outside the model whereas others can. And outside the model they do just what

---

[116] Van Fraassen 2018.
[117] Williams 1986.

our usage expects of them: they help fix what is to come. Here I adopt J.L. Mackie's idea of *fixity* as central for the identification of *causes*.[118] For the purposes I focus on, what is special about the facts that we label 'causal' is that *causes help fix the open future.*

Powers

Happily for us, this often happens in predictable ways, either naturally or because we have engineered arrangements that have just the characteristics where our predictions are reliable. To mark this, I have long talked about nature's *capacities,* but since my capacities are similar in many ways to the powers that many metaphysicians and a few philosophers of science now embrace, I shall here use the more usual term 'powers', as I have done in chapters 1 to 3. Massive objects have the power of gravitational attraction; charged objects, the power of Coulomb attraction and repulsion. As I argued in chapter 2, this does not mean that there is something in the world anything over and above the massive object and what it does. *The ascription of a power to an object in virtue of features it possesses marks out a complicated pattern of facts about what happens when those features act in a variety of arrangements.* Masses influence accelerations of massive objects; charges influence accelerations of charged objects. When mass and charge act together on a body in a specific arrangement, so long as nothing else influences its acceleration, what happens is predictable in the well-known way, as in Millikan's famous oil drop experiment where the charged droplet hovers motionless while pulled down by gravity and up by an electromagnetic field, a result we reliably predict from

$$a = (\mathbf{F}_G \oplus \mathbf{F}_C \oplus \mathbf{F}_D)/m$$

where m is the mass of the droplet and $\mathbf{F}_G$ and $\mathbf{F}_C$ are the familiar functional forms $GMm/\mathbf{r}_{Mm}^2$ and $\varepsilon qQ/\mathbf{r}_{Qq}^2$ that we label 'the force of gravity' and 'the Coulomb force', with $\mathbf{r}_{Mm}$ the vector distance between the masses and $\mathbf{r}_{Qq}$, that between the charges.

'So', you may ask, 'what is a power?' That is a wrong question given what I am trying to do with powers. Unlike the metaphysicians, I am not interested in discovering fundamental ontology but rather in understanding scientific practices; in this case, particular theoretical practices that we use

---

[118] Mackie 1974.

to predict outcomes and build devices. As we see in the Millikan example, we associate labels with various qualities and quantities and have learned ways to use these labels to predict what objects with these qualities and quantities will do with respect to particular kinds of outcomes in particular kinds of arrangements. To the extent that things go as we envision, we have discovered a kind of systematicity in nature. These qualities and quantities are different, in ways we rely on, from other features for which we know no such methods and, for which, perhaps, there may be no systematic behavior. These are the features that I classify as 'powers', like the power that being charged brings to a body to attract or repel other charged bodies. This marks that there is a reliable, albeit complicated, systematicity to outcomes that these features affect.

Hedged Predictability

It is important to note though that the predictability is heavily hedged. In a very controlled arrangement like Millikan's the acceleration is predictable. But what happens when other things that we have no idea how to represent in a Newtonian equation also influence the acceleration? Perhaps a small earthquake shakes the lab. Then the acceleration is not predictable. And for all we know, it may not be predictable in principle. Nature may, as the title of this book notes, be an artful modeler; she may follow no rules for exactly what will happen then. The causes acting together fix the acceleration, but it is not set in advance just what value they set it at. It is because of this possibility, even in this highly physics-regulated setting, that I talk of causes fixing the *open* future.

Determinism

This brings us to the vexed issue of determinism. As Mackie notes:

> The further analysis, in terms of fixity and unfixity, could have objective application provided only that there is a real contrast between the fixity of the past and the present and the unfixity of some future events, free choices or indeterministic physical occurrences, which become fixed only when they occur. Now we certainly do not know that there are no such events; we do not know that strict determinism holds; but neither do we know that it does not.[119]

---
[119] Mackie 1974.

I realize that, unlike Mackie, many philosophers feel we must assume strict determinism: 'That's what science shows.' But that is far from the case. The conclusion that the universe is deterministic is a big leap—a *very* big leap— beyond what the evidence of the successes of our sciences more readily supports. True, we make use of equations, like those involving time derivatives in physics, that fix the values of some variables at one time from values of others at an earlier (or later!) time. But our successes in using these do not even provide evidence that the very outcomes represented in those equations are always determined, and that's so even supposing these equations are the best ones to use to generate those successes.

I express my last remark as I do because I am an instrumentalist with respect to these equations, regarding them, as I argued in chapters 1 to 3, as 'symbolic representations': These equations are not propositions, so they cannot be true or false, and plausible renderings of them as propositions cut against their usefulness. But I am probably in the minority here; most of you may think in terms of scientific laws that can be read literally and that we would like to be true. Intuitions that science locates us in a deterministic universe are fed, I believe, by our tendency to conflate distinct characteristics that these 'laws' of science might have, as Pedro Merlussi and I explain in chapter 6. Using L to label some set of correct laws for our universe (supposing we can make sense of that idea), for our purposes here Merlussi and I distinguish two things:

> *Extent.* Is every kind of thing that happens covered by L? For instance, there may be whole domains of happenings about which L is silent. And this may be true for even the complete set of laws for our universe (if such there is).
>
> *Permissiveness.* When L speaks about the outcomes that are to occur at some later time, given facts about an earlier time, what kind of latitude does it admit? For instance, does it select a single happening? Does it lay down at least a probability, or can L admit a set of different outcomes, remaining silent about their probabilities?

The issue regarding *extent* is simple and probably will be familiar. There may be situations where the laws are silent; they simply do not cover those situations. For instance, L may be deterministic in the sense that for each appropriate input regarding earlier facts, L admits one and only one output to occur, yet L is limited in extent because some real situations do not fall into any of the categories for the kinds of past facts that L uses to calculate future facts.

Permissiveness is less familiar I suppose. Laws may be permissive in at least two different ways. They may allow a range of outcomes and set a probability over them, as we see in quantum theory. Or they may set a range of outcomes with no probability. Once we have admitted that it is consistent with lawful behavior that some events in the purview of laws may just happen—by hap—as in quantum mechanics (where on occasion it just *happens* that this electron showed spin up on measurement as opposed to spin down), there seems no reason that events cannot happen by hap with no frequency fixed for how often which occurs. Perhaps this is an even easier case to envision since it is, after all, difficult to make sense of how nature manages to get the frequencies right across all those different cases.

Think about another case similar in structure to the Millikan experiment with the small earthquake. An earring-back is stuck in some debris in the crack between the floorboards. You try to lift it with a magnet. The magnet has the power of attraction. We may suppose it pulls upward on the metal object with a fixed strength we know how to write down and feed into the Newtonian equation we use to calculate acceleration—similarly with gravity pulling it down. But the debris also inhibits the motion of the earring-back. Maybe the debris has features, like mass or charge, with systematic powers, like that of gravity and Coulomb attraction and repulsion, so that there is a function to add into the Newtonian equation to calculate the motion of the earring-back. But certainly 'being debris' is not a feature with a power like that. And maybe the debris has no such power. To assume it must because it can affect the motion of the earring-back is to make a massive metaphysical assumption beyond the empirical evidence.

I use this example because it involves the simple, and so reliable, physics that we know and love, and yet it is so typical of our everyday experience where, even if there is relevant physics to bring to bear—unlike most situations we need to manage in life—there's not enough physics to predict. There could be hidden and secret physics, I agree. But my commonsense, Missouri empiricism tells me to suppose the world is pretty much the way I experience it to be until there is very good reason to the contrary. And the multitude of successful uses of those physics equations in highly special, 'shielded' arrangements (and then generally with lots of ad hoc corrections), gives weak warrant indeed for the conclusion that there are bigger and better equations somewhere in God's heaven to fix outcomes that are properly in the range of the equations, like accelerations, let alone everything else, like whether the dishwasher will wash the dishes this evening.

Whence possibility then?

Recall the words of Ruth Barcan Marcus quoted in chapter 2:

> An actual chess player in an actual game has alternative moves of which he selects one. . . . it is difficult to deny such unactualized moves an objective status. The alternatives can be precisely described and many of their immediate consequences traced. Such examples can be multiplied. Alternative experimental outcomes, partially completed projects, 'generate' possibilia of great specificity. They are not merely in the mind or vagaries of fancy. They present themselves publicly and are clearly identifiable.[120]

Possibilia are a natural consequence of a combination of systematicity and permissiveness in the happenings in nature. There is enough system to mark out what is possible but not enough to single out one particular outcome. Recall those possible fat men in the doorway discussed in chapter 2. How many are there at this moment, assessed from, say, two minutes ago? As I argued before, that has an answer, though I don't know it. It depends on how far which men were located from the door and whether the range of their locomotive powers included walking fast enough to get there in time.

Returning to van Fraassen

Bas van Fraassen allows that there are possibilities in models but then asks: '[W]hat corresponds to the elements of this sort of model, in reality, in nature?' He answers: '*Only what actually happens.*' There is little in the story I have told about possibilia that is all that contrary to what van Fraassen desires, or for that matter to the demands of those who urge a Mill-Ramsey-Lewis (MRL) account of laws in which things happen but they *just* happen; they just happen to happen the way they happen, albeit, happily for us, they happen in patterns that laws summarize. This MRL view is more or less what I have presented, only without the law summary commitment since I think these patterns are *very* complicated and that our representation of these patterns lies in our modeling *practices*: We capture specific instances with purpose-built models that we have used power ascriptions to construct.

---

[120] Marcus 1975-1976, 43.

So perhaps causings are a bigger sticking point than possibilia. I say that causings help fix the open future. I find it hard to deny that since I see it happening. The way the cat is lapping up the milk is disappearing the milk in front of my eyes. The magnet, the debris, and gravity all act together on my earring-back. The outcome is open, though constrained. In situations like this, things like the earring-back sometimes stay stuck; they sometimes move about a little but not enough to retrieve it; they sometimes rise up, stuck to the magnet. But they do not turn into a pumpkin. That's the point of talking of powers—it marks out the set of outcomes that do happen when features like this act together. Though the outcome is open at the start, as these three features act together in this particular setting, some possibilities drop away—aha, now the magnet has a really good grip, it is pulling the earring-back right along, now it is rising. . . . We can see the outcome being produced by this process.

Van Fraassen has talked in the past about how the theories we use affect how we see things. We both agree about that. My confidence that the magnet helped fix the outcome is aided by my theory about the power of magnetic attraction. So I see that the magnet is lifting the earring-back in part on account of the theory. But that does nothing to show that what I see isn't there in the world to be seen.

Conclusion

Like van Fraassen, I suppose that there is *'only what actually happens'*, just a small fragment of which is represented in the model. And for the kind of empiricist I am, as with the kind he is, that means just the actual happenings, with, as he says "nothing at all in nature to 'ground' the other possibilities or the constraints on those possibilities." I offer nothing to ground them and like van Fraassen, I don't see which things that happen need grounding and which don't. Yet I still cannot see why among the actual happenings we do not have causings and possibilia. The cat does really lap up the milk and, as of two minutes ago, there really were three fat men who could possibly have been in the doorway now.

5

Big Systems versus Stocky Tangles: It Can Matter to the Details

1. Introduction

Wolfgang Spohn and I have discussed causation for a long time, very often disagreeing on the details: do causes increase the probability of their effects, does the causal Markov principle hold for all 'complete' sets of causal relations, is there one concept of 'cause' or many, are there only as many causes as needed to reflect the probabilities or many more, does the concept of direct causation make sense, and more. We also have very different philosophical viewpoints and concomitant methodologies. What I had not realized till working on this commentary on Spohn's so-well-deserved Frege Prize lecture is how much the little, local disagreements are connected with the big differences.

Spohn's work is a tour de force, an impressive edifice of formal argument to produce a model world. I by contrast follow a piecemeal approach. What I hope to do here is to show how these big-picture differences can underpin real differences in the philosophical details, using causality to illustrate. This is not in aid of arguing for one approach or the other, nor for one stand or another on this or that issue of causality but rather to see better how local disagreements converge with broad methodological differences.

I am an advocate of the Stanford School, which I characterize by: pluralism, particularism, and concern with practice. The Stanford School is epitomized for me by Patrick Suppes's demand: "Let's get down to the details." I couple that with Suppes's—and Spohn's—insistence on rigor. But Spohn and I differ on where the rigor lies. My particularism bans idealizations that make things look the same only by not looking very carefully, and the commitment to practice keeps my arguments low to the ground. Also, consonant with Stanford School particularism and pluralism, comes skepticism of "the big system," which marks a clear divide between Spohn and me. What I worry about *the big system* is reliance on long arguments and lofty generalizations.

In a *long argument* with many separate premises, the conclusion fails if any of its premises fail. No step in one of these arguments is likely to be entirely uncontroversial; each is at least a little dicey. The probability, then, that one or another, somewhere along the line, is false is significant. So why should we trust the conclusion, even if we cannot spot where the error lies? It is on account of this concern that I oppose

> Tall, skinny arguments that are sparse and tidy

In favor of arguments that are

> Short, stocky, and tangled.

'Stocky' is wide—the arguments cover a lot of the territory under the conclusion—and solid. I use 'tangled' to describe a rich network of interrelated arguments, each firmly attached to the ground, some with shared premises but where a great many also have a number of independent premises and, importantly, premises that come from a variety of different places outside the immediate domain in which the conclusion lives. Long, tall arguments can be beautiful, elegant, an intellectual triumph. But where security of conclusions matters, we had better stick to arguments that are short, stocky, and tangled.

Lofty generalizations. My view about lofty principle is much like Pierre Duhem's of the laws of physics. They are rough templates; they organize a great deal of material under them—so long as you don't look too closely at the details and you avert your gaze from items that you might have wanted to cover in the first place but that don't fit into the box. Lofty principles do an essential job of organization for us; and they are often great tools for beginning to build accurate models. But when it is security we want in our conclusions we should look far closer to the ground.

By contrast with the construction of the big system, this piecemeal particularism may look very unphilosophical. For instance, Pierre Duhem tells us about some of the British ancestors of this tradition:

If the mind of Descartes seems to haunt French philosophy, the imaginative faculty of Bacon, with its taste for the concrete and practical, its ignorance and dislike of abstraction and deduction, seems to have passed into the lifeblood of English philosophy. "One by one, Locke, Hume, Bentham, and the two Mills[. . .]" All these thinkers proceed not so much by a consecutive line of reasoning as by piling up of examples. Instead of linking up syllogism, they accumulate facts. (Duhem 1906, 67)

Locke, Hume, Bentham, and the two Mills: these are paradigms of Suppes's injunction to get down to the details.

Let us look now at issues of causality to see how these general philosophical differences can crop up again and again, shaping concrete philosophical conclusions at a local level.

2. Getting Hold of Causes

Let us call the world of objects in states of affairs that Spohn constructs—i.e. his 'totality of facts'—the 'projected world'. Independent of whether there are unprojected objects doing things and independent of whether Spohn's epistemically-based pragmatic theory of truth can save him from idealism, I do not agree with Spohn about the status of causation in his projected world. Spohn undertakes a grand Kantian construction to end up with a Humean world—a world where causation is literally 'not to be seen'. It is not there among Spohn's states of affairs, let alone among those states of affairs that are facts. (Facts, recall, are the states of affairs we arrive at in the ideal limit of inquiry.) That's why he needs the excursion into reasons to get causality and other, as he terms them, 'modal facts in the ordinary sense, i.e. . . . the so-called natural modalities' (Spohn 2016, 13).

Everything but the one concrete universe is for Spohn an epistemic projection, but causation is an epistemic projection within an epistemic projection. There are objects and states of affairs within Spohn's projected world, but which kinds of states of affairs? His is a strange under-populated world, devoid of all causings as such. There are no pushings; no pullings; no teachings or learnings; no smotherings or uncoverings; no eliminatings or restorings; no gratings, choppings, bakings, whiskings, sauteeings, boilings; no beheadings, invadings, executings, enslavings, or freeings; no helpings nor hinderings; electings nor just taking charges, . . . These are all causings in the general sense proposed by G.E.M. Anscombe, that a cause produces or is responsible for its effect (Anscombe 1971); the cause makes the effect happen; the effect comes out of the cause, which is, I would argue, what is in common among the various happenings that we want to label 'causal' for various purposes in various settings. They are all causings and no causings exist in this projected world.

We may, as Spohn allows, assign a truth value—indeed the truth value 'true'—to 'Nancy caused the boulder to fall'. But not because any actual pushing by me can be found in our projected world. Rather because Nancy [but what feature of Nancy if not her pushing?] is a reason for the falling of the boulder, a conditional reason 'given the entire history [of that world] up to' (Spohn 2016, 16) the falling of the boulder. Nor does causality supervene on some complex of facts. In particular, although Spohn is responsible for significant advances in work relating causality to networks of facts about probabilistic dependencies and independencies, causal claims are not summaries of any complex of facts about objective probability relations.

Spohn is surprisingly like Bas van Fraassen, who, as we have seen in chapter 4, also puts causal facts in a special category, a step beyond even theoretical entities. Spohn trades eventually in ontology whereas van Fraassen's concerns are consistently epistemological, with what rationality permits and compels belief in, and correlatively with what knowledge science should provide us with. But both arrive at a three-tier society, each tier less respectable than the one before, with my poor friend, Ansombian causality, relegated to the outermost circle.

This is a new level of epistemic projection. As Spohn says, "It is entirely subjective; what speaks for what is determined by my subjective epistemic state or, more specifically, by my conditional degrees of belief" (Spohn 2016, 15). Spohn tells us, "Since reasons are relative to an epistemic state, causation is so too . . ." But, as he urges, "causal judgements involve very special beliefs: given the entire history up to t, what do I believe to happen at t" (Spohn 2016, 17).

This relativization to an entire history is important. It is an essential ingredient in Spohn's escape from idealism. The other essential ingredient involves laying down some principles about the nature of causal reasoning, Spohn's 'objectivization conditions of causal beliefs'. Once these assumptions are in place, he can show that his dynamic theory of inductive inference—his theory about how reasons for changing one's beliefs work—becomes a theory of causal inference. He tells us in *Laws of Belief*:

> The causal relation is just the objectifiable part of our much richer and more disorderly reason relation. In other words, if we want to objectify our inductive

strategies, if we want to align our dynamics of belief to the real world, we have to attend to causation, to the objectifiable part of our reasons. This is what the notion of causation is for. (Spohn 2012, 469)

Let us look more closely at this reasons relativization. It is familiar in epistemology to suppose that reasons are reasons for agents each with their own peculiar background beliefs. But Spohn needs something stronger than the usual relativity of reasons to background beliefs. For his purposes the verdict about reasons must depend on a specific set of background beliefs: those about the entire history of the world. This calls into play a very special agent, one with beliefs about that entire history. But it is not enough that the agent have beliefs about what the entire history of the world is, those must be *true*. If not, Spohn's truth conditions give the wrong results. So I think we need to read Spohn thus:

SC: x causes y iff x is a reason for y for an agent who believes H is the history of the world up to the time of y AND H is the history of the world up to that time.[121]

This may seem like minutiae, but it matters when it comes to real, on-the-ground, practical epistemology: how can we actually go about finding out about the world? In judging that x causes y we must, à la Spohn, judge whether x would be a reason for y given that one knows the entire history of the world. That's a tall order! To be fair, it is not as tall as may at first appear. For this does not require one to know the entire history but merely to judge what would be reasons if one did. That may not be at all impossible.

By now most philosophers will be familiar from the work of Gerd Gigerenzer and others with the idea of a 'cheap heuristic'[122]—a method of thinking through a problem that gets one to the right end point (or near enough often enough) without going through a laborious 'brute force' calculation. Moreover we know we don't need to look at the entire history of the world to make a reliable causal judgment. Our standard comparative methods in the sciences look for differences between the presence and absence of causes controlling for a far smaller domain of features:[123] the other causes

---

[121] An anonymous referee underlines that it is not the agent who knows the whole history who is to judge that x is a reason for y but 'us theoreticians'.

[122] Cf. Gigerenzer et al. 1999.

[123] Consider for example a later replication of a physics experiment to test a causal hypothesis. What matters is that the other causes for the effect are the same, or accounted for, not any further information about the intervening history of the world. This is also assumed

operating to produce *y* at the time. If *x* is a reason for *y* once we know those, then *x* is a cause of *y*. So we call into play Principle CC, which I present in its crudest form, for simplicity of discussion:[124]

> CC: *x* causes *y* iff *x* is a reason for *y* for an agent who knows all the other causes influencing *y*.

CC, I claim, is the lesson that probabilistic theory of causality teaches and it is the justification that lies behind our standard scientific methods for causal inference.[125]

Why does Spohn not use CC rather than SC from the start? The answer for conventional Humeans is that they want to offer a reductive account of causation: necessary and sufficient conditions for '*x* causes *y*' that refer only to facts in a 'Hume world', i.e. a world where states of affairs consist of objects exhibiting some special kind of non-modal properties. CC judges whether *x* causes *y* relative to other causes of *y*. The Humean can avoid relativizing to other causes by relativizing to the whole history of the world, which is bound to catch all other causes.[126] Spohn's motivation is similar:

> The crushing conclusion [from CC] is clear: any explanation of the circumstances must refer to the notion of causation. The circle is vicious... We stand at a crossroads here. Should we continues to strive for an explication of the notion of causation that results in an explicit [reductive] definition?... I am heading for the more ambitious project. (Spohn 2012, 355)

Things may not be so bad between CC and the Humeans as they first appear however. CC constrains labeling the relation between *x* and *y* 'causal' by how the relations to *y* of other features are labeled—are these labeled 'causal' or not? But CC equally constrains whether the relation between any

---

in our use of statistical methods for testing causal claims, like stratification (we stratify on other causes and take that to be sufficient if it could be done), randomized controlled trials, qualitative comparative analysis, causal-Bayes-nets methods, and instrumental variables and other econometric methods (in these latter the 'exclusion' conditions refer to other causes, not to arbitrary factors in past history). The assumption is also clear in J. L. Mackie's (1974) famous and widely adopted INUS theory of causality from which at least the claim that causes are INUS conditions is widely adopted though not the converse).

[124] Both Spohn and I adopt something along these lines. Not surprisingly, our two versions are different.
[125] Cf. Cartwright 2007, ch. 3, "Causal Claims: Warranting Them and Using Them."
[126] This supposes that relativizing to more than we need does not change the verdict.

other feature, say z, and y is labeled 'causal' by whether the relation between x and y is labelled 'causal'. CC thus acts as a consistency constraint on the full set of relations labeled 'causal' with respect to y.

Consistency constraints can be a powerful tool, as we see from their use in various sciences. For instance, the first serious quantum theory of the laser (by Willis Lamb) relied on a 'self-consistency' model. Perhaps more familiar are rational expectations models in economics, which demand that the mean values that agents in the model predict for certain quantities (i.e. the agents' expectations in the sense of what the agents anticipate will happen) are the same as the mean values for those quantities that result from the agents' actions (i.e. the expectations of those quantities in the statistical sense). This consistency constraint, coupled with other principles in the model, fixes the behaviors of the agents uniquely.

Unfortunately CC by itself is not enough to dictate a unique verdict about what sets of features are causally related. But there are further constraints on the causal relation we could adopt that would do the job. This is what I see Spohn's objectification conditions doing. If causal relations are to satisfy this extended set of constraints then, given our pre-settled reasons relations and the way the world actually is, there is only one verdict possible about whether x causes y for each pair of features $<x,y>$.

This however creates a puzzle for me about why Spohn opts for SC rather than CC. He after all (unlike me) is inclined to accept his objectification conditions—and these, if I understand them correctly, operate essentially on CC not SC. Moreover, adopting SC creates a special demand given that the narrower CC is sufficient. Because now a defense is required that SC implies CC. This involves showing at least three things. First, that the huge amount of extraneous information contained in the entire history of the world never produces a different verdict than the narrower information about what other causes influence y. Second is a consistency condition, that CC for x causes y follows from SC for x causes y supposing that SC is used in CC as the criterion for whether or not each other factor is a cause of y. Third, when SC is used as a criterion for judging which are the 'other causes' to be used in CC, it gets them right.

Connecting with CC is no idle matter, especially if one starts from a concern with the real epistemic practices that get us around in the world.[127] CC is at the core of our many methods for causal inference that depend on

---

[127] This discussion is foreshadowed in footnote 121, which was added in response to a call by an anonymous referee to expand at that point.

Mill's method of difference, including both 'single-shot' controlled experiments and methods that look for probabilistic differences, as in econometric causal models, stratified observational studies and randomized controlled trials. Consider a 'single-shot' controlled experiment to see if x causes y: we fix, to the best of our ability, the other causes of y, then look to see if the presence versus absence of x makes a difference. Here we have not only epistemological and manipulability problems with employing SC but it is literally impossible for the entire history up to y to be the same in the settings with x and without x.

Supposing we do require that SC imply CC. There are three strategies one can pursue to defend SC. The first is argument by philosophical example. This however is better suited for showing that things are not equivalent than for showing that they are. It also suffers from the well-known problem that intuitions about what verdicts are correct in various cases differ and can depend heavily on the context to which a case is assigned in the process of evaluation.

The second strategy is to establish an empirical connection. Here we face the general problem that Hasok Chang labels 'the experimenter's regress' (Chang 2004): We want to see whether A, which we know how to find out about, is a good indicator of B, which we don't: is CC a good indicator of SC? But we can't establish a correlation because we have no way to figure out when B holds in the first place. This is a standard problem in developing measurement procedures in the sciences where we use a variety of methods together in an ongoing feedback process to solve it. For instance, where there's some reasonable starting theory of the sources or the consequences of B, we look to see if those occur in the face of A. We also look for convergence among the verdicts of different indicators each of which has some starting plausibility. But these strategies are not so promising for the case of SC and CC.

First, because in the sciences we often evolve our notion of A—for example, just what temperature is—in tandem with refining the details of the Bs that are supposed to be indicators of it. This wouldn't serve to defend SC as it is, and modifying SC would threaten the impressive network of proofs that underwrites Spohn's account of causality.

Second, I don't see how to carry it off. What corresponds to the empirically testable sources or consequences of the set of factors judged relevant by SC that might correlate with CC's relevance set? Or, what other methods are plausible starting methods for identifying the SC relevance set that might converge in their verdicts with the CC method for doing so? We can agree, I believe, that there are many cases where a variety of different kinds of indicators that x caused y converge, and converge with the verdict of CC (indicators like the character of the effect [does y occur at the time, in the manner and of the size to be expected had x caused it?], various symptoms of causation [e.g. side effects that could be expected had x operated to produce y], the presence of requisite support factors [moderator variables] and absence of inhibitors, and the presence of expectable intermediate steps [mediator variables]). The problem is to provide some reasonably good starting argument that these are connected with SC.

The third method is proof, and here Spohn has something incredible to offer: a series of proofs that "instead of the largest possible circumstances . . . [NC: i.e. the entire history of the world] we may as well base our explication of direct causation . . . on much smaller [sets of] circumstances . . . and thereby arrive at exactly the same direct causal relations" (Spohn 2012, 373). Here different smaller sets will recoup slightly different kinds of direct causes. None of these are exactly CC, which Spohn does not believe is always correct,[128] but under one special assumption that he thinks can often hold, SC causal verdicts will be the same as those of CC.

Why am I still worried? Because I don't see how to satisfy my third desideratum: that we have reason to think the causes picked by SC are correct. How can I doubt that, given that, for purposes of this discussion, I have assumed that CC gets it right? My reason lies in one of the strengths of the proof itself: it does just what I said is demanded for consistency, which is to show that SC implies CC, where the 'other causes' referred to in CC satisfy SC. But I want them to satisfy CC and it seems we need this very proof to show they do. This is perhaps fixable by some kind of expanded proof by induction. So I move to my more general worry, which returns me to the overall theme of short and stocky versus tall and thin.

The argument is too long—way too long, and many of the premises are controversial. Let's start at the end of the chain. We don't get a unique verdict from SC about whether x causes y without additional assumptions. The central ones Spohn employs are close relatives of the three central axioms

---

[128] Though for different reasons than mine for modifying CC. Mine depend first on the fact that there are a variety of other reasons than common causes why two factors may be correlated, whereas CC deals at base only with common causes (e.g. x may be a reason for y even once common causes have been taken into account if they are produced in tandem by a probabilistic cause; or if they are joint causes of the same effect in a population where that effect is universally present; or if they change in the same direction in time); second, because x may cause y but not be a reason for it, for instance where its positive effects on y and its negative balance. Cf. Cartwright 2007, chapter 6, "What is wrong with Bayes nets?"

characterizing causal Bayes nets. Quite independently of Spohn's use of them for objectification, I have quarreled with every one of them ... and for separate reasons.[129] For each there are, I maintain, many sets of relations that we wish to label 'causal' that do not satisfy that axiom. Not only do we wish to apply that label to these relations but doing so does real work for us of one kind or another that we expect of causal relations, like helping to assign responsibility and blame, or to predict what will happen, to understand the world better, or to change it.

I do not suggest that I and others are right in all our criticisms of all these Bayes nets axioms. The problem is that they make for a very tall argument for objectification. All these objections and counterexamples could be wrong. But that seems extremely unlikely; and, if they are not, there's a reasonable chance that one of these premises is not a universal condition on causation. If so, objectifivization is out the window unless or until other arguments are to hand, and I would want *lots* of other arguments to make the whole structure far more stocky.

Looking back further, there is Spohn's theory of reasons to buy since assumptions about how reasons operate are essential for the theory of causation, both for the proof that SC implies versions of CC and for the proof of uniqueness that turns epistemic causes into objective ones. Here again one can have quarrels with specific assumptions but what I would like to draw attention to is a kind of relativization in the theory of reasons that endangers the objectification of causation: the relativity to choice of model. Although the relativity of causes to reasons may be eliminated by a successful uniqueness proof, no such proof is in the offing for model-relativity, as Spohn himself notes: cases of causality are always described by a "(conceptual) frame" that specifies the set of variables to be used (Spohn 2012, 341). Ranks and probabilities, which formalize reasons for Spohn, both require event spaces to range over, as does the notion of the entire history of the world used in defining direct causation. Further, the concept of direct causation requires dividing time into discrete chunks so that nothing can get in between a direct cause and its effect. Verdicts relative to one formal frame can differ from those relative to another, as Spohn stresses in his 1990 paper, 'Direct and Indirect Causes'. This paper relies on probabilities rather than the ranks of his 2012 *Laws of Belief* but the treatments of causality in the two are parallel. Spohn explains:

---

[129] Cf. Cartwright 2007 and Cartwright 1999.

everything said about causation is relative to the descriptive frame given by the [event space] . . . [This relativization] is essential because the causal relations may indeed vary with the frame. (Spohn 1990, 125)

When this can happen, the objectification constraints can pick only a set of causal relations that are unique up to the choice of frame, which is no objectification at all.

Some frame relativity can be shown to be harmless. Sometimes it doesn't matter whether we fine-grain or coarse-grain the event space and sometimes expansions and contractions do not matter. But these kinds of results are not sufficient to eliminate frame relativity.

Perhaps, though, following ideas from Spohn's pragmatic theory of truth on the limits of scientific exploration, "where absolutely everything is explored" (Spohn 2016, 12), we can hope that the self-correcting methods of science will tend towards a unique choice. After all, Spohn tells us, "In the limit of inquiry not only our beliefs are guaranteed to be true; we also know what the states of affairs and what the facts are" (Spohn 2016, 13). Spohn's work on the dynamic laws of belief has certainly made impressive inroads on the formal and philosophical side to, as he puts it, "develop [the pragmatic theory of truth] so as to meet theoretic standards" (Spohn 2016, 12).

The problem is that I find little in the practices of the sciences to support this hope. For me the job is not to make sense of the (in Spohn's terms) "nice metaphoric" (Spohn 2016, 12) of 'the limits of inquiry' but rather to see that such limits make sense for real inquiry into the real world. When we get down to the details, as Suppes urged—the details of practice—rather than convergence I see ever more unrelated proliferations of event spaces from different subdisciplines looking at not only different problems and different aspects of them but often looking at what appears to be the same aspect of the same problem but with a different methodological slant.

Of course the limit is traditionally described as the 'ideal' limit to abstract from the details of the real. That's okay so long as *idealization* is what Catherine Elgin calls a 'felicitous falsehood' (Elgin 2012). A felicitous falsehood puffs up the truth about features of interest and lies about many others in order to highlight the characteristics we care about and eliminate ones that mask them from us. But it has its feet firmly in the actual; it cleans up what is there, presents it in a better light. It does not whisk away the actual and drop something more desirable in its stead. This latter kind of idealization, which is closer to what we see in Spohn, does not support Spohn's project of objectivization.

But perhaps Spohn would insist it does. For in discussing speculation about "general, or the most general, laws of belief" that are "at best loosely connected with empirical facts," he claims: "it is certainly desirable to conceive the manifold of relevant phenomena under some general laws, even if only as idealizations that apply to reality only with massive help from correcting theories" (Spohn 2012, 7).

This echoes my own view, and that of many instrumentalists and pragmatists (and notably Duhem whom I have quoted) about the general laws of high physics theories. Conceiving the phenomena under these laws, even if they only apply with massive corrections (which, I have argued, practice shows is the only way they apply), is indeed desirable, and for a host of reasons. The general laws provide an all-purpose tool that, when used with the right other tools in the right ways, case-by-case, can help in the construction of close-to-the-ground models that apply with hardly any corrections. And, as Mary Morgan points out in her work on the travel of facts and techniques from one domain to another, seeing that the more low-level laws grouped together under the same general claim are similar in significant ways allows us to use similar methods of study, modeling strategies, approximation techniques and the like and it suggests analogous predictions to look for from one domain to another (Morgan 2009).

So in the sciences, idealizations that fit the world only with massive corrections can be useful for many purposes. But I don't see how this kind of idealization can serve Spohn's aims, either with respect to objectifying laws of nature or for the project under discussion here of achieving an appropriate event space for the objectivization of causes. If we are to base things that matter about the world on what is arrived at in the limits of scientific exploration, "where absolutely everything is explored," should that not be in the limits of exploration as we actually engage in it when we are successful in finding out about the world—or at least seem to be successful judged by our most rigorous criteria?

To support convergence in the face of my practice-based worries, one might turn to our successful 'high' theories in physics or perhaps biology. I say 'high' theory because that is where we might expect both to overcome proliferation and to find convergence. Can the concepts these theories employ provide the requisite event space and can this be expected to converge on some limit in the end of inquiry? The answer I think is 'No' to both. Consider convergence first. Physics high theory has an exciting history, a monument to the human imagination in part because it has exhibited such dramatic changes in the kinds of features it introduces. That is an old theme from the history of science, much discussed, especially in the US, in the 'science wars' of the 1990s. So I'll say no more about it here.

What about the event space itself? Can it overcome the problems of proliferation? No: the very virtue that leads us to turn to it makes it unfit for the jobs Spohn undertakes. For the event space supplied by high physics theory will not include the bulk of the actual causes that make things happen in the world. I note three strands of practice-based argument in support of this pessimistic conclusion.

The first is short. Physics theory consists of equations and there are no causes to be found in these equations. I myself have argued against this, as have Mathias Frisch and others (Frisch 2012). But it seems we are in the minority. I won't rehearse the arguments on both sides. I just note that in case Frisch and I are wrong, this presents a real challenge to the hope to turn to physics theory for an event space in which causes can be objectified.

The second argument is one I have developed in a paper in memory of Lorenz Krueger (Cartwright 1998). When it comes to producing outcomes in the real world, or describing how they come about, even ones where our knowledge of high physics theory plays a central role, we utilize mixed, untidy collections of concepts from a wide range of sources, including engineering, ordinary good sense and hands-on tacit knowledge of how things work together. Even the physics comes from many different, narrow, unorchestrated special subfields. Physics may be the Queen of the disciplines but she does not dictate what happens; she is only part of a motley assembly. We can try to idealize away the motley assembly but then we lose the ability to predict and control. Or we can assume that the ways we produce and explain outcomes will be very different in the future than they have been in the past. But I see no grounds for betting on this.

The third argument has to do with the way physics concepts hook onto the world. Here is one picture. The concepts used in producing and explaining real outcomes only look motley because we are looking at too concrete a level. It is well known that things that look different in the concrete may be the same in the abstract. The trajectory of a coin falling to the ground, of a planet circulating the sun and of a cannonball shot over a moat may look different at that level of description but they are in fact all motions subject to a central gravitational force. If this view is a plausible idealization (in the good sense) of what is going on, then maybe the single event space can be salvaged.

But I don't see any way to defend it in the face of the empirical record. My particularism here follows two heroes of mine, Otto Neurath and J. L. Austin. Neurath pointed out that the exact concepts of proper science do not fit the blousy empirical world in which we conduct the business of producing outcomes and explaining why things happen. For most of the concepts we use in causal reasoning, we have no idea how to relate them to those of physics. Even for those we connect with physics, it takes a lot of additions and subtractions, a great many of which are ad hoc. They are there just to bend the concepts of physics to fit the phenomena. This is part of the reason that the laws of physics fit onto the world only with massive corrections and it was Neurath's reason for rejecting the project of theory of confirmation to substitute the looser notion of shaking. Empirical results cannot confirm or dis-confirm theory in actuality; they can only shake or steady our confidence in it.[130]

Austin was similarly suspicious of the attempt to sweep everything into one tidy space:

> This is by way of a warning in philosophy. It seems too readily assumed that if we can only discover the true meanings of each of a cluster of key terms . . . that we use in some particular field (as, for example, "right", "good" and the rest in morals), then it must without question transpire that each will fit into place in some single, interlocking, consistent conceptual scheme. Not only is there no reason to assume this, but all historical probability is against it. . . . We may cheerfully use, and with weight, terms which are not so much head-on incompatible as simply disparate, which just don't fit in or even on. Just as we cheerfully subscribe to, or have the grace to be torn between, simply disparate ideals—why must there be a conceivable amalgam, the Good Life for Man? (Austin 1956–1957, 29, note 16)

I have here no new arguments for the proliferation of concepts necessary to do causal reasoning. That is the meat of my book *The Dappled World*. But I had not before seen how those views, grounded in the demand to 'get down to the details' and to look at the practices of knowledge acquisition and use in contrast to the promissory notes, intersects so consistently with Spohn's project. The difference in basic philosophical method seems reflected in specific disagreements at many unexpected internal points.

---

[130] Cf. Cartwright, Cat, Fleck and Uebel 1996.

3. No Causes In, No Reasons Out

I focus on causes not only because it is where Spohn and I have met most often but because I fear that the failure of causes to appear in Spohn's projected world from the start undermines his plan to procure them via reasons. For, I urge, there are no reasons without causes, or more accurately, without some forms of what Spohn calls 'natural modalities', like causes, laws, powers, or perhaps Stephen Mumford's dispositional modality.

Why? A reason for y must, as Spohn says, 'speak for' y. But it must also be able to speak *to us*. This latter causes trouble. But let's start with the former. This is what I call 'evidence' in my theory of evidence for policy and wheresoever rigor matters.[131] Whether (the fact referred to by) x speaks for (that referred to by[132]) y or not depends on what else is true. That is why I picture evidence as a 3-place relation: x speaks for (is evidence for) y relative to argument A iff A is a valid argument for y with true premises and x is a premise in A that is essential for the derivation of y. This a very non-restrictive notion of evidence since there are always valid arguments that turn any actually occurring fact into evidence for any other. If x and y are both true then so is $x \supset y$ and thus x is evidence for y relative to an argument for y with x and $x \supset y$ as premises.

I don't think this is harmful for a general account of evidence. x does speak for y relative to the truth of $x \supset y$. If you know $x \supset y$, then surely finding out that x holds is a good way to find out that y does. But can x thereby be a reason for us for y? That depends (at least) on whether $x \supset y$ could be available to us. We can learn x is true but that is no help with respect to y if the only way to access $x \supset y$ is by learning y. There are facts about the world that will do the job, facts that—if we can learn them at all—we can learn without directly learning y. And I would argue that we can learn them since we are never in possession only of data in Spohn's sense, though that is not necessary to my point here. For if we cannot, then even these facts cannot salvage reasons. What matters is that these all involve some one or another of the natural modalities. For instance, if there is a law that y follows x, or it is true that x causes y, or that they share a common cause, or that x and y are jointly sufficient and separately necessary causes of some further fact z that obtains, or x is 'disposed' to y in Steven Mumford and

---

[131] See Cartwright 2013 and Cartwright and Hardie 2012.
[132] For simplicity of presentation I shall hereafter drop attempts to avoid use/mention conflations.

Rani Lill Anjum's dispositional modality sense (Mumford and Anjum 2011), then there is some truth about the world that could supply access for us to $x \supset y$ without having to learn y. But not otherwise. And that seems a real problem for Spohn's programme.

Spohn wants to build what he calls 'an inductive scheme': a "scheme that projects from each possible sequence of data some set of beliefs"; and he wants to do so in the 'normative mode', in which "we want to know which inductive scheme is the right one" (Spohn 2012, 3). One scheme we know is not the right one is induction by simple enumeration: Swan 1 is white, swan 2 is white, swan 3 is white . . . So the swans in Sydney Harbour are white. But every scheme that relies only on patterns in a sequence of data is essentially induction by simple enumeration.

We can look to the work of John Norton, which was discussed in chapter 1, to support my concerns about inductive schemes. Norton has a two-pronged argument. First he raises problems for the most plausible schemes he can identify. Second he describes what he thinks is actually going on in real life scientific inductions in his 'material theory of induction': "inductive inferences are not warranted formally but materially. They are justified by facts . . ." (Norton, manuscript 2014, 2). And the material facts that do this job turn out to be modal.

We can get a good idea what this involves from what Norton calls 'the clearest illustration', Marie Curie's induction on radium chloride:

> The attempt to explicate it with the schema of enumerative induction failed. We could not justify why the schema should be limited precisely to the few properties of radium chloride that Curie so confidently generalized. The justification for this restriction cannot be found in any formal analysis of predicates and properties. Rather, it lies in the researches of chemists in the nineteenth century. The core result is known as "Haüy's Principle" . . . [which] asserts that, generally, each crystalline substance has a single characteristic crystallographic form. The principle is grounded in extensive researches into the chemical composition of crystalline structures and into how their atoms may be packed into lattices. That means that once one has found the characteristic crystallographic form of some sample of a substance, generally one knows it for all samples.
>
> Curie's inductive inference is warranted by Haüy's Principle and not by conformity to any inductive inference schema. There is an inductive risk taken in this conclusion, as indicated by the "generally" in the principle. (Norton, manuscript 2014, 10)

The first thing to note is that although, as Norton indicates, there is inductive risk—Haüy's principle may have exceptions, what matters is that Haüy's principle is just that—a principle. Exceptions will have explanations. Second to note is that Norton takes Haüy's Principle to state a material fact. Third, that it is a natural modality. The principle does not just describe some pattern that has help in the data. If it did, the inference would after all be in accord with familiar inductive schemes. It depends rather on the nature of radium chloride, on the nature of other chlorides and on further chemical principles:

> We now know that all crystals fall into one of seven crystallographic families ... Discerning these families constituted a major mathematical challenge and it was only after the mathematical problem was solved that truly reliable inductive inferences on crystalline forms were possible. When Curie identified radium chloride crystals as just like those of barium chloride, she was adopting the expediency of not specifying the family formally, but merely allowing that it was the same as that of barium chloride. This in turn lent credence to her induction since another principle of chemistry, the law of isomorphism, allowed that analogous chemicals formed similar crystals. (Norton, manuscript 2014, 10, 11)

As in this case, in all of Norton's examples the material facts that support inductive inference turn out to include natural modalities, like 'Generally, each crystalline substance has a single characteristic crystallographic form' or 'Electrons all have the same size charge'. So in Norton's scheme, as in mine, there are no reasons without modalities.

Is this not just Hume's problem of induction then? If so, this should not assuage the worries I have been raising. Hume's argument is very clever. He like Spohn constructs a Hume world, a world without any of the natural modalities. Then he formulates a problem about reasons that cannot be solved without modalities. That problem is a problem for us only if the Hume world is a good model of ours, or, to be more fair to Hume, of our world as we can experience it. But the Hume world is not a good model for ours and there are no compelling arguments that it is once Hume's doctrines about what impressions are, his copy theory of ideas and his accompanying associationist theory of concept formation are rejected, as I take it they should be.

Our world, even as we experience it, is rife with modalities. One might argue, following Wilfrid Sellars, that if we can know that objects have specific properties, we must already have access to some natural laws. That's because properties—like being a radium or a barium chloride crystal—come in families with natural behaviors and natural relations to other properties. We must recognize these if we are to know that we have radium chloride crystals in front of us, even if like Marie Curie, what we know is but a crude version of the natural connections so we are not able to "specify the family formally." A similar conclusion is suggested by the now popular metaphysical doctrine that properties are collections of powers, so that, in whatever sense one knows that an object has a property, one must know that it has at least some of the salient powers that constitute that property.

These are both deep and controversial issues about topics that I do not study in detail. I touch on them to point out that the modality close to my heart, causality, is not alone in its claim to be a part of Spohn's world of facts. There are independent arguments for other modalities to be there as well. My own favorite is causality, which brings me to the question of my last section: Where did all the causes go in Spohn's projected world?

Before that though I should consider one way to try to solve the problem of how to have reasons without first having causes yet in the same breath maintain that we cannot have causes without reasons. That is: reasons (i.e. good reasons) and causes are co-constituted. They are built together. This is an exciting prospect, and a project of a kind that Spohn is a virtuoso at. We are not there yet but perhaps he will get us there. Curmudgeonly me of course would probably not be happy even then because of the idealizations I suspect such a proof would involve, "idealizations that apply to reality only with massive help from correcting theories."

4. Where Did All the Causes Go?

Why do we need an account of causality at the point that Spohn proposes one for? Once we are moving in the projected world, why can we not use the simple Tarski formula for its truth conditions, supposing that the right-hand-side is evaluated at the projected world: 'c cause e' is true iff c causes e, just as Spohn can presumably use this for other relations (like 'a is larger than b' is true iff a is larger than b)?

Spohn tells us at the start

- "The world is a collection of facts."
- "The universe is just one big concrete object."

- "Universes are concrete objects... whereas totalities of facts are very complex states of affairs (or collection thereof)" (Spohn 2016, 3).

Here is an alternative more attractive to the practical, particularist heart.

- There are a lot of objects. (Notice though that I do not say *a collection* of objects.)
- They are different. Some are big, some little, some negatively charged, some positively, some are electrically neutral, etc. It seems they may differ in more far more ways than we can imagine or that can be counted.[133]
- Things happen, objects change, objects interact. The ball falls to earth, little children grow big, brightly colored sweaters fade in the wash, electrons attract protons, cats lap up milk.
- To get one big concrete object takes work, for instance, like that described by Erhard Scheibe (Scheibe 1991). He claimed there was just one big concrete object. His argument was roughly this. Physics tells us that everything interacts. But under physics laws, if two things interact, they are no longer subject to evolutionary laws separately but only evolve together. So ultimately there is only one thing subject to the laws of evolution: the whole interacting lot. Scheibe's argument may get us to the conclusion that there is just one big object but it won't serve Spohn's purposes since what it shows is that (supposing laws like the current ones in physics are correct), there is only one object *for physics laws to evolve*; the laws can't evolve the different objects separately. It does not get us Spohn's universe as 'one big concrete object'—indeed, the only *concrete* object—from which other objects appear only under projection.

I urge this alternative as the background for my assumption that the world—even if projected—comes much as it looks to us and much as we describe it, with causings right there along with what (I take it) Spohn would include under the label 'data'. Taking the world as it comes until provided with convincing evidence that it is some other way is part of my Stanford School pragmatism, where the evidence should look much like what we would demand of evidence in real practice. If, with the projection of objects and properties, we arrive at a world with states of affairs and facts, what principle allows in facts that fall under the label 'data' but not a huge swathe of the facts that I see around me?

---

[133] Note that I follow Bas van Fraassen's stricture and do not say 'there are properties and objects differ by which they have.' Nor do I say 'properties are collections of objects'.

Presumably there are relations among Spohn's properties. Why then the relations 'a is to the left of b', 'a is bigger than b', 'a is redder than b' but not 'a pushes b', 'a smothers b', 'a restores b', 'a bakes b', 'a helps b', etc. These relations are, as Anscombe argued, observable and a great many are measurable, as I argue in *Nature's Capacities and Their Measurement*. We can also provide informative characterizations of what they are and describe how they relate to other relations. I do not see how to mount an argument that once we have projected facts we have not already projected causings. So there seems no need to use reasons as a tool to get causes into the (projected) world. This is all to the good since, if my worries are borne out, there would be no reasons available for the job in a world without causings.

5. Conclusion

I have focused on the effects of broad differences in philosophical viewpoint to show how big differences can affect local quarrels. The point is to show what these broad differences can amount to when we get down to the actual philosophical work. Neither Spohn nor I would want to urge that one of these viewpoints should be pursued at the cost of the other. Surely at least this pluralist conclusion is correct: philosophy needs both.

6

Are Laws of Nature Consistent with Contingency?

Nancy Cartwright and Pedro Merlussi

1. Introduction

Are the laws of nature consistent with contingency about what happens in the world? That depends on what the laws of nature actually are, but it also depends on what they are like. The latter is our concern here. Different philosophic views give different accounts of the sort of thing a law of nature is. We shall look at three that are widely endorsed: 'Humean' regularity accounts, laws as relations among universals, and disposition/powers accounts. Our question is, given an account of what laws are, what follows about how much contingency, and of what kinds, laws allow?

Of the three types we shall look at, powers stand out as especially apt for admitting contingency, or so it would appear from conversations we've been engaged in, both with powers advocates and with powers opponents. Our investigation here suggests that this is not so. A powers account of laws may admit contingency but it need not. Conversely, the other accounts may rule out contingency but they need not. In all three cases, we shall argue, the root idea of what laws are does not settle the issue of whether they allow contingency. Advocates of the different accounts may argue for one view or another on the issue, but (at least as we understand the accounts) this will be an add-on rather than a consequence of the basic view about what laws are.

Here we explore the possibility of various kinds of contingency in nature, contingency despite the pockets of rough order we observe in our daily lives and of precise order we report in our modern sciences. But, are contingency and order not obviously in opposition? Yes, we think they are–*if* a picture of nature dominant since the Scientific Revolution is correct, that order arises from the rule of universal deterministic laws, laws that hold everywhere and everywhen and that cover all aspects of what happens. But, we shall argue, that picture is not dictated by any of the three kinds of accounts of laws we investigate. Contingency and order are not in conflict on a 'Humean' regularity view of laws, as we describe in Section 2. They are also not in conflict if the source of order in nature is relations among universals, as we discuss in Section 3, nor if it is powers and dispositions, neither on Alexander Bird's version nor on that of Nancy Cartwright and John Pemberton. Cartwright and Pemberton argue from how much of modern science works; Bird, by contrast, approaches the issue with the questions and perspectives of metaphysics. We shall briefly review his account in Section 4; in Section 5 Cartwright, following consultation with Pemberton, develops various ways in which contingencies are possible on the view of powers (which they call 'capacities') they advance.

We shall assume for this discussion that whatever laws of nature are, they are the kinds of things that our current best science might be representing—not that our current science has it right but that we don't want our philosophic doctrines about what kinds of things laws of nature are to rule out that the world is pretty much as current best science pictures it. In particular, then, we want to admit that candidate accounts of what laws of nature are should allow at least this: whether a radioactive atom decays in some given period of time is contingent, though the probability of this happening is not.

Clarifying the question. Whether contingency is possible given the laws of nature depends not only on what kinds of things laws of nature are but also on what contingency consists in. We distinguish several different questions one might ask in asking 'Do the laws of nature allow for contingencies in nature?'[134] To be as neutral as possible we shall talk of laws *covering* a happening P if they, along perhaps with what the view of laws on offer counts as the 'right' kind of facts (boundary conditions, initial conditions, facts about the past, etc.), say that P will happen (as is typical with common accounts of

---

[134] We should note that we are not concerned with what the actual laws allow but rather with what laws allow by virtue of the kinds of things they are. It may be, for instance, that a particular account allows that laws may be either deterministic or probabilistic but that the actual laws are all deterministic.

deterministic laws) or that it is allowed to happen (as with common accounts of probabilistic laws). Using *L* to label the complete set of correct laws and $P_0(L,P)$ for the additional facts that bring L to bear on P, here are the questions we want to keep sorted from one another.

Extent. Is everything that happens covered by L? For instance, there may be happenings, or kinds of happenings, or whole domains about which L is silent.

Permissiveness. When L speaks about the outcomes that are to occur, what kind of latitude does it admit? For instance, does it always select a single happening? Does it always lay down at least a probability, or can L admit a set of different outcomes, remaining silent about their probabilities?[135]

Reliability. Does what L (plus some relevant $P_0(L,P)$) says is to happen always happen? For instance, can there be exceptions to L and yet L still be the correct and complete set of laws?

Potency. Do the things that L speaks about happen on account of L? Or, for instance, merely in accord with L?

Free will. If P, which happens, is an action of a person, is ~P consistent with $P_0(L,P)$ (whatever might be the appropriate $P_0(L,P)$) obtaining and L being the correct and complete set of laws?

We introduce the last question because it hovers in the background. Indeed, it is one of the things that motivated the thinking behind this chapter: Merlussi is otherwise writing on the consequence argument in metaphysics (to be discussed in Section 2), which begins with a version of determinism to argue to the conclusion that nobody ever could have done anything to make P false, for any P that describes human actions; and it is often suggested in conversation with Cartwright and Pemberton that a capacities account of laws like theirs leaves more room for free will than other accounts. *Free will* is, we all know, a huge question to which over millennia an enormous amount of intense thought has been dedicated, involving of course debate over the very formulation of the problem. Still, we think there are some simple observations we can make about how some accounts of laws of nature bear on the aspect of the question we formulate here.

We will not always have much to say about every question with respect to each view of laws we survey but rather focus on what might not be altogether obvious or on where interesting differences lie. We will not address *potency* seriously at all. It is generally supposed—though not without objections—

---

[135] We propose treating laws that say 'anything goes' in some circumstance as not covering that circumstance and thus limited in extent.

that universals and powers accounts allow for *potency*, as well as accounts that involve 'necessary' regularities, whereas 'Humean' regularity accounts do not. We shall not take up this issue because we have nothing useful to add. We list it for completeness and to make clear that it is a separate issue from the others.

There are two guiding ideas we rely on throughout in considering *extent* and *permissiveness*. The idea for *extent* is simple: There may be situations where the laws are silent; they simply do not cover those situations. This is an issue, we claim, that is orthogonal to questions about whether laws are *permissive* when they do speak. For instance, L may be deterministic in the sense that for each appropriate $P_0(L,P)$, L admits one and only one P to occur, yet limited in extent because some real situations are not $P_0(L,P)$-type situations for any admissible $P_0(L,P)$, i.e. some situations may not fall into any of the categories for the additional facts that bring L to bear.

With respect to extent, a little simple housekeeping is necessary since some of the discussion in both the philosophy of science and the philosophy of religion literature as well as in the related metaphysics literature is confusing (at least to us) because it does not make clear the formulations at stake to begin with, especially with respect to the quantifiers and what they range over. Consider the claim G': 'Politeness requires giving an expensive gift to one's teacher/mentor,' that we suppose is true in some cultures influenced by Confucianism. Shall we say it is limited in extent, or shall we rather consider G: 'In cultures A,B,C, politeness requires giving an expensive gift to one's teacher/mentor,' which is, we suppose, true everywhere and in that sense not limited in extent? Similarly, Cartwright has suggested that what we think of as the usual laws of physics L' may well be limited in extent in a very specific way: They may be unable to represent all the possible causes of the effects they represent; their truth may then be restricted to just those cases where only causes they can represent are at work.[136] Thus, it should more perspicuously be formulated something like this. L: 'So long as all of the causes of the consequences represented in L' are features represented in the antecedents of L', then L'.' One could think of formulating the issue in terms of domain restrictions: Are these restrictions included in the laws themselves or not? The problem is that it can be difficult to formulate criteria for what counts as a restriction on the domain of a law versus what counts as a feature that it genuinely covers. This is why we formulate the issue as we do: Are there things that happen that the complete and correct set of laws does not cover?

---
[136] Cartwright 1989, 2009, 2010.

Are Laws of Nature Consistent with Contingency?

As to *permissiveness*, although we turn to capacities last, it is useful to foreshadow one of the topics discussed there because it will help with understanding our remarks about permissiveness throughout. Cartwright has long urged that some events, even ones in the purview of laws, may just happen—by hap—without even any probabilities assigned by nature. Recall the example from chapter 4. An earring-back is stuck in some debris in the crack between the floorboards. You try to lift it with a magnet. The magnet pulls upward on the metal object with a fixed strength and gravity pulls it down with a fixed strength. These activities are both properly treated as sources of forces, where by 'properly' she means that there is a general way to ascribe forces for both. There is a magnet and there is a rule in physics for what forces magnets exert; and there is a large mass—the earth—and there is a rule for what force a mass exerts. There is also debris that inhibits the motion of the earring-back. Maybe there is another description of this particular debris for which there is a proper rule in physics that assigns a force. But certainly not under the description 'debris.' And maybe there is no other such description. We may grant that some causes of motion are forces in the proper sense of that concept but that does not imply that all are. To assume there must be because the debris can affect the motion of the earring-back is to make a massive metaphysical assumption beyond the empirical evidence, Cartwright argues.

If we leave the issue open, then a new possibility for contingency arises. There is a rule for what force is exerted when the magnet and the earth act together in this arrangement, and on this rule only one resultant force is allowed. But what about the motion of the earring back? Is there a rule that says what one motion will happen in this arrangement when the resultant force of the earth and the magnet acts on the earring-back simultaneously with the inhibiting efforts of the debris, or if not a rule dictating one single outcome, is there a rule that dictates a set of outcomes with a probability measure over them?

We have insufficient reason to assume there is, as was argued in chapters 1 through 3, so that assumption should not be forced by our account of what laws are; the account should leave the question open. Yet surely there is some kind of rule since we have what do seem well-warranted beliefs that the earring-back will not fly away at near the speed of light, and also, as Keith Ward[137] has pressed, that it will not turn into a pumpkin. This is very underexplored territory. But it seems that here may lie yet another source

---

[137] Personal conversation with respect to Cartwright and Ward 2016.

of contingency; we have labeled this *permissiveness*: When L applies, given a relevant input $P_0(L,P)$, L might admit only one outcome, in which case L is not permissive. On the other hand, L may be permissive in that L admits a set that includes more than one outcome, and in the latter case, L may or may not provide a probability over that set.[138]

2. The 'Humean' Regularity Account

The central motivating idea behind what we shall call the 'Humean' regularity account of laws is not about laws but about the make-up of the world. The facts that constitute the world involve only qualities, quantities, and relations that are *occurent*, where 'occurent' means different things to different philosophers who call themselves 'Humeans.' What they all have in common is that they, like van Fraassen and Spohn discussed in chapters 4 and 5, want to exclude any kind of 'modal' features. There are no causings, no necessitatings, no doings, no making-things-happen-ings.

In answer to the question 'What is it to be a law of nature?' the naïve 'Humean' account states that laws are regular associations among occurent features. But this is thought to be problematic. There are true accidental regularities that are not laws, it is supposed. To use Hans Reichenbach's memorable example, 'All gold spheres are less than a mile in diameter' is a genuine regular association, but this does not seem to be a law.[139] So, it is commonly assumed, a satisfactory 'Humean' view of laws should distinguish laws from accidental regularities. This is what David Lewis's best system account (BSA) sets out to do.[140] Since BSA is very well developed and widely adopted, we shall focus on this version of the 'Humean' regularity account. However, the main arguments we put forward should go through for any acceptable 'Humean' account of lawhood, including Craig Callender and Jonathan Cohen's 'Better Best Systems Account.'[141]

In *Counterfactuals* and "Humean Supervenience Debugged," Lewis takes as a starting point a short note written by Frank Ramsey in 1928.[142] Lewis's restatement of Ramsey's passage asserts that 'a contingent general-

---

[138] Clearly this supposes some already given way to individuate outcomes.
[139] Reichenbach 1947, 368.
[140] Lewis 1973.
[141] Cohen and Callender 2009.
[142] Lewis 1973, 73, and Lewis 1994, 478.

ization is a *law of nature* if and only if it appears as a theorem (or axiom) in each of the true deductive systems that achieves a best combination of simplicity and strength.'[143,144]

Notice two important features of this view. First, laws supervene on the particular matters of fact. This is so because laws merely summarize facts. So, as to *potency*, laws do not 'govern' the world, they are just special regularities that encompass a good many other regularities. The particular matters of fact determine the laws of nature in the sense that if the laws of nature are different, that's because the facts are different. Because of this, the BSA preserves the alleged intuition that the laws of nature are metaphysically contingent, at least so long as it is metaphysically contingent what the facts are.

Given this brief description we can look at how the BSA deals with questions of whether L is compatible with contingencies.

Extent. Does L cover everything that happens? Following John Earman, one might formulate the question as follows: Do laws have an unrestricted range in space and time?[145] As Earman points out, to deny that laws have an unrestricted range in space and time boils down to saying that there is 'a region of space-time R_o such that, as far as L is concerned, 'anything goes' in R_o.'[146] More precisely, where M denotes the set of all models of the putative law sentences, this may be formulated as the question of whether claims representing the complete and correct set of laws L satisfies the following condition:

---

[143] Lewis 1973, 73. This looks like a use/mention confusion but it is almost certainly harmless. We shall try to avoid confusing the two but occasionally for ease of expression we will follow Lewis in talking in the formal mode when the claim is really one in the material mode.

[144] Here's what this means: Consider a true deductive system in which the general claims that represent laws of nature appear as a set of true sentences T that is deductively closed and whose non-logical vocabulary contains only predicates that express occurent properties. There are many ways systems can be axiomatized. If the axioms of T preclude more possibilities than T, 'then T is *stronger* than T.' Likewise, some true deductive systems can be axiomatized more simply than others, in the sense that they have fewer axioms. The general claims representing the laws of nature will belong to all the axiom systems with a best combination of these two virtues, simplicity and strength.

[145] Earman 1978, 174.

[146] Earman 1978, 174. We use this formulation because readers may be familiar with it. But there is no reason to assume that nature thinks in terms of space-time regions rather than, as in Cartwright's view, in terms of what features obtain. For instance, as we noted, her rendering of boundaries on the range of a theory T is roughly this: Those instances of effect E that T covers are the instances for which some or all of the causes of E fall under concepts available in T.

(U) There is no non-empty, proper subregion R_0 of space-time such that for any M ∈ M, there is an M' ∈ M where M' ⊨ L and M'|$_{R_0}$ ≈ M|$_{R_0}$,

where the symbol ≈ stands for model isomorphism and M|$_R$ denotes the restriction of M to R.

This condition states that L is valid on a model that is not restricted to some spatio-temporal region, that is, L is 'universal.' Given the BSA there is motivation for thinking that the laws of nature should be 'universal.' If the range of the axioms (or theorems) of the best deductive systems were limited to some spatio-temporal region, then one would expect more axioms to summarize the whole history of the world. That is, one would need more axioms to cover all spatio-temporal regions. But if the range of the axioms is not limited, then one can naturally expect fewer axioms to summarize all the particular matters of fact. Furthermore, this will not reduce the system's informativeness, since the axioms now are not restricted to some spatio-temporal region. On the other hand, if nature is fairly unruly outside a given range, adding piecemeal information about what happens there to any set of axioms may increase informativeness at too great a cost to simplicity. So the laws may be limited in extent. Despite the fact that the BSA explains why we might expect the laws of nature to be universal, it seems that Earman is right in saying that there is no a priori guarantee that the laws of nature according to the BSA will satisfy (U).[147]

Permissiveness. Within its domain, under the BSA, does the correct L (plus relevant initial or boundary conditions) always single out a unique outcome? In order to answer this question one needs to bear in mind the main motivation behind Humeanism about laws. The world is void of modalities—no causings, no necessitatings, no probabilifyings; the world is nothing but a mosaic of occurent events. Laws summarize what happens in this mosaic, rather than 'governing' what the particular matters of fact are.

If L is deterministic, given an appropriate P_0(L,P), L admits only one outcome. But there is nothing in the Humean motivation that makes determinism natural. The best summary may be provided by purely probabilistic laws or by laws that constrain outcomes to a given set but do not choose among them nor lay a probability over them. As Helen Beebee points out whether the world is best axiomatized under deterministic laws depends on how regular the world is.[148] The world can be modality free and still irregular enough to be summarized best by non-deterministic laws.

---
[147] Earman 1978, 180.
[148] Beebee 2000, 575.

Reliability. So as not to muddle together issues of *extent, permissiveness,* and *reliability,* let's consider the most difficult case for contingency in the *reliability* sense: where the laws have universal extent and are deterministic, allowing only one output for any relevant input. It looks at first sight as if in this case on the BSA, they must be reliable. There can be no exceptions to the correct laws. We think, however, that there is still some wiggle room and will offer two ways that might be thought sympathetic to the 'Humean' viewpoint that might allow for exceptions, one of which is due to Lewis himself. For the sake of this discussion we propose to adapt Earman's definition of determinism in terms of possible worlds to define deterministic laws because it makes for a ready connection to the Lewis wiggle.

Let $\mathcal{L}$ stand for 'L is the correct set of laws,' then define 'deterministic' thus:

Laws L are *deterministic* iff for any P that L covers and any $P_0(L,P)$ that is 'appropriate' input to L for P and any logically possible worlds w, w' in which $\mathcal{L}$, if w and w' agree on $P_0(L,P)$, they agree on whether P obtains.

An interesting way to address the question of the reliability of deterministic laws under the BSA is by considering Scott Sehon's objection to the standard definition of determinism.[149] First, we start by pointing out that

D: If $\mathcal{L}$ and L is deterministic then for any P that occurs and that L covers and any $P_0(L,P)$ that occurs that is an appropriate boundary/initial condition for P with respect to L, $\square((P_0(L,P) \,\&\, L) \supset P)$.

To see why, suppose that L is deterministic and $P_0(L,P)$ is an appropriate boundary/initial condition for P with respect to L and P. Let W stand for the collection of all possible worlds. Consider an arbitrary world w in W where $P_0(L,P)$ and L. Because L is deterministic, if P obtains in any world where L and $P_0(L,P)$ obtain, it holds in all worlds where $P_0(L,P)$ and L obtain, including w. P obtains in our (the actual) world where L and $P_0(L,P)$ obtain. So P obtains in w and thus $(P_0(L,P) \,\&\, L) \supset P$ in w. Since w is any arbitrary possible world, $\square((P_0(L,P) \,\&\, L) \supset P)$ follows.

Sehon, however, thinks that this is problematic. He argues that L and $P_0(L,P)$ should allow exceptions. Even if the correct laws are deterministic, Sehon claims, it should be logically possible that there is, for example, an

---
[149] Sehon 2011.

interventionist God (IG) that could miraculously change water into wine.[150] As Sehon says, 'necessarily, if an IG exists, then it is possible that the same initial state of affairs obtains, along with the same laws of nature, and yet P is false'—i.e. it is possible that $P_0(L,P)$&L&~P.[151] His reasoning can be spelled out as follows (using IG to stand for 'There is an interventionist God'):

1. $\Box(IG \supset \Diamond(P_0(L,P)\&L\&\sim P))$ Premise.
2. $\Diamond IG$ Premise.
3. $\Diamond(P_0(L,P)\&L\&\sim P)$ From 1&2, assuming S4.
4. $\sim\Box((P_0(L,P)\&L)\supset P)$ From 3.

And (4), clearly, is the contradictory of $\Box((P_0(L,P) \& L) \supset P)$, which follows from the assumption that L is deterministic.

Note that Sehon's main point does not depend on the premise that an IG is logically possible. One might try to cast Sehon's objection as a call for a domain restriction: L holds everywhere that there is no interventionist God (L holds if ~IG). 'Humeans' might not like this because there is no way that the domain restriction could be brought into the antecedents in the laws of nature since laws are supposed to involve only occurent features, and God's intervening does not seem a good candidate for an occurent feature on any 'Humean' account of 'occurent' we know. That aside, the problem is that determinism would be incompatible, say, with the logical possibility of an interventionist demon, in the sense that, necessarily, if an interventionist demon exists, then it is possible that $P_0(L,P)$&L&~IG&~P. So, Sehon's main worry is not about the logical possibility of an IG, nor about the logical possibility of a demon in particular. It is about the logical possibility of the laws of nature being violated.[152] Thus, Sehon urges, exceptions to what L (and $P_0(L,P)$) say should happen should be possible even if determinism is true, precisely because it must be logically possible to violate the laws. And if the BSA does not accommodate that, there must be something wrong with the BSA as an account of laws.

In what follows, we will show how a Lewisian might reply to this argument, showing that the BSA may be consistent with assuming that the correct laws are deterministic and yet can be violated, at least in a sense. The task then is to show that these two propositions are consistent:

---

[150] Sehon 2011, 31.
[151] Sehon 2011, 31.
[152] A domain restriction in this case seems to make law claims tautological, which they should not be for the Humean: 'As are regularly associated with Bs except when they aren't.'

p: The correct laws L are deterministic.
q: It is possible to violate (the correct laws) L.

The first strategy is to hedge on *p*, using Lewis's own notion of soft determinism, which is supposed to allow a sense in which agents are able to do things such that, if they were to do them, what L says happens does not happen.[153]

Let us assume the truth of *p* and thus of **D**, so that some statement about the distant past, $P_0(L,P)$, and L logically imply, for instance, P: 'Agent A did not raise her hand.' What if A had raised her hand? There are three options:

1. If A had raised her hand, contradictions would have been true.
2. If A had raised her hand, $P_0(L,P)$ would be false.
3. If A had raised her hand, L would be false.

Someone like Lewis will naturally reject option 1. Even if the agent had raised her hand, contradictions would not have been true. Lewis also denies 2. Even if the agent had raised her hand, the past would still be the same, so $P_0(L,P)$ would still be true.[154] Thus, if we want to say that the correct set of laws L is deterministic and sometimes we are able to act otherwise, the only option remaining consistent with Lewis's viewpoint is 3. Thus, given $P_0(L,P)$ and **D**, ~P implies L is false. Yet, we are supposed to be arguing that L are the correct laws. How is that possible? Following Lewis the clue is: correct in what worlds?

To see how this works we need to draw a distinction between two senses in which one can violate a law:

> *Weak sense*: An agent is able to do something such that, if she were to do it, a law would be violated, either a law of the actual world or a law of nearest possible worlds.
> *Strong sense*: An agent is able to do something such that, if she were to do it, a law would be violated and this law would be of the actual world.

For example, in the weak sense, if the agent were to have raised her hand (i.e. we assume she did indeed raise her hand in the actual world), contrary to what L says, then L would have been violated before the hand raising. To use Lewis's phrase, a 'divergence miracle' would have happened before

---
[153] Lewis 1981, 114.
[154] Lewis 1979a.

that, that is, there would be a violation of the laws of nature that hold at our actual world, and this violation would not be caused by A's action. Note that to say that there is a violation of the laws of nature in the weak sense is not to say that the violated laws are the laws of the same world where they are violated. The term 'miracle' is used to express a relation between different possible worlds. As Lewis says, 'a miracle at w_1 relative to w_0, is a violation at w_1 of the laws of w_0, which are at best the almost-laws of w_1.'[155] So with a divergent miracle in our actual world, whose laws are the 'almost' laws of a nearest world where L is not violated, we can violate the correct laws of that nearby world. Or vice versa. Now, if by 'violating a law' we mean the weak sense where what we violate is an 'almost law,' not a real law, of our world, then it seems agents may be able to violate laws that are deterministic.

But what if by 'violating the laws of nature' Sehon means the strong sense? The *strong sense* is the one in which the laws are violated in the actual world that are the laws of the actual world. This seems what Sehon has in mind when he says that, if IG, then it is possible that we have the same laws, the same past, and yet P is false. However, if by 'violating a law' Sehon means the strong sense, then someone like Lewis will deny that it is logically possible to violate a law in the strong sense. This is so because, as Lewis says, 'any genuine law is at least an absolutely unbroken regularity.'[156] Given the BSA, it is clear why we cannot violate laws in the strong sense. Suppose it is a law that no object moves faster than light. If someone were to throw an object that moves faster than light, then that law would not be true. Since Lewis's 'Humean' laws are true regularities, if it is a fact that a certain stone moves faster than light, then it cannot be a true regularity that no objects travel faster than light.

'Humeans' might, however, consistent with the commitment that there are only the occurent facts of which laws are summaries, take a more instrumentalist line. The best summaries may not be required to be true, especially if this brings about a big gain in simplicity. They could admit of exceptions but be right most of the time. Or they could be wrong most all the time yet still very nearly right most, even all, of the time. This is like William Wimsatt's view that laws could be templates that fit widely but in many cases not exactly.[157] Whether admitting false claims as the correct laws is a good idea on the 'Humean' view depends on what the world is really like. Cartwright

---

[155] Lewis 1979a, 469.
[156] Lewis 1981, 114.
[157] Wimsatt 1992.

Are Laws of Nature Consistent with Contingency? 123

has argued that high-level laws in physics often get fitted to the real details of real situations only by adding ad hoc corrections.[158] That could be because we have just missed out on the factors that support those corrections and that bring the situation genuinely under the laws. But it could be that that is just what the world is like. There is no single uniform pattern but only a template which fits widely but not very exactly (or as argued in chapter 1, that doesn't really fit at all but plays a role in constructing a model that does fit fairly well—though this would not support reliability in the sense intended in BSA). If the latter is the case, the BSA can be maintained while allowing contingency in the *reliability* sense, so long as the demand is given up that the best summary of the facts be true.[159]

Potency. Do the things that L speaks about happen on account of L? Or, for instance, merely in accord with L? Perhaps this is the least problematic question to answer according to the BSA. Clearly, the things that L speaks about happen merely *in accord* with L.

Free will. The question whether the 'Humean' account of laws plus assumption **D**, which follows from the hypothesis that the correct laws are deterministic, is compatible with the possibility of agents doing other than what they do, can be introduced in the context of the currently central argument for incompatibilism,[160] namely the *consequence argument*.[161] One of the crucial premises of the consequence argument is that the laws of nature are not up to anyone. The modal formulation makes use of a modal sentential operator '■' in which '■P' abbreviates 'P and no one has or ever had any choice about whether P.' '■' is supposed to satisfy these two inference rules:

(α) $\Box P \vdash \blacksquare P$
(β) $\blacksquare(P \supset Q), \blacksquare P \vdash \blacksquare Q$.

Here is the consequence argument, supposing that L are the correct laws, the correct laws are true, P is something that happens, and $P_0(L,P)$ is the relevant feature to fix P given L:

---

[158] Cartwright 1983.

[159] Here it is easy to make things look simpler than they are by blurring use/mention distinctions. If laws are 'false' but 'nearly true' then the laws will not be facts as we first claimed for BSA but rather only very similar to facts.

[160] Incompatibilism here understood is the view that if determinism is true, there's no free will.

[161] Cf. Ginet 1983 and van Inwagen 1983. The Consequence Argument is so called because it relies on the *consequences* of the laws of nature and the past in order to establish incompatibilism.

1. □ ((P₀(L,P) & *L*) ⊃ *P*) from determinism.
2. □ (P₀(L,P) ⊃ (*L* ⊃ *P*)) from 1.
3. ■ (P₀(L,P) ⊃ (*L* ⊃*P*)) from 2 and rule (α).
4. ■ P₀ (L,P) premise, fixity of past.
5. ■ (*L* ⊃ *P*) from 3, 4, and rule (β).
6. ■ *L* premise, fixity of laws of nature.
7. ■ *P* from 5, 6, and rule (β).

Is premise (6) true? One might interpret the '■' operator in a more precise way as follows:[162]

(■-*def.*): ■P if and only if P & ~∃x ∃α [Can(x, α) & (Does (x, α) □→ ~P)]

where '□→' stands for the counterfactual conditional, x ranges over agents, and α ranges over all past, present, and future action types.

The idea is that there is nothing that anyone can do such that if they were to do it P would be false. Now, is '■L' true according to this interpretation? As the interpretation above makes explicit use of a counterfactual conditional, and since we are interested in seeing how the 'Humean' might answer this question, the natural way to proceed is to use an account of counterfactuals that is in line with the BSA. So we will presuppose Lewis's own semantics. At a first approximation, let us say that

(C-L): A □→ B is (non-vacuously) true in a world *w* iff B is true in all the worlds in which A is true that are closest to *w*.

Given (■-*def.*), if '■L' is false, then some agent *s* is able to perform an action *a* such that, if *s* were to perform *a*, then L would be false. To put it in a different way, is L true in all the closest worlds in which P: Agent *s* does action *a*? Suppose ~P, that *s* does not perform *a* in the actual world w_0. Now, suppose worlds in which *s* performs *a* have the same laws as the actual w_0 and these laws are deterministic Can we consider these worlds to be the closest relative to w_0 among the worlds where s performs a? Since worlds in which *s* performs *a* do not agree on P they cannot agree on any P₀(L,P) that with L determines P nor on any R(L,P₀(L,P)) that with L determines P₀(L,P), and so forth. Now L—the set of complete and correct laws of our world—may be very limited in extent. Perhaps they only cover P, in which case the only fact

---
[162] Pruss 2013.

besides P on which these worlds disagree with the actual is $P_0(L,P)$. But this won't work if they are to account in the way we usually expect for the amount of order we see in the world. For instance, what about all the knock-on effects from all the initial or boundary conditions that are related under L to P? And the knock-on effects of the Rs that need to be different when all the laws in L are deterministic to ensure the P_0s are? When so much divergence from the actual world, w_0, occurs in these worlds, can these worlds be the closest worlds relative to w_0 in which s does a? Following Lewis's own maneuvers in cases like this, the better option, it seems, is to regard as 'closest' those worlds that are just like w_0 up to about the time that s performs a, and then diverge by a divergence miracle. Therefore, the closest worlds in which s performs a are not worlds in which the same laws L obtain. Therefore, the 'Humean' who follows Lewis has motivation for considering '■L' false and, consequently, for rejecting premise 6 of the consequence argument.

3. Laws as Relations among Universals

Fred Dretske, Michael Tooley, and David Armstrong developed a rival approach to the BSA.[163] In what follows our presentation will focus on Armstrong's view. Laws of nature, according to Armstrong, are necessary relations among first-order universals. The ontological component of a law according to the BSA is a regularity; on Armstrong's view, it is a second-order relation between first-order universals. Suppose that all Fs are Gs and that the laws of nature ensure this. F-ness and G-ness are taken to be first-order universals. Armstrong states that a second-order contingent relation holds between these two universals. He labels this relation as 'nomic necessitation' and he uses 'N' to refer to it. Armstrong symbolizes the relation of necessitation between F and G as 'N(F,G).' He also claims that the holding of N entails the corresponding generalization. If the second-order relation N holds between the first-order universals F and G, then 'N(F,G)' entails 'All Fs are Gs.'

On the traditional Armstrong/Tooley/Dretske view it seems that laws are *reliable*—what they say goes, goes. At least this is the case under the assumption at the core of the view[164] that the relations that obtain between universals make true the corresponding relations between instantiations

---

[163] Dretske 1977, Tooley 1987, and Armstrong 1983.
[164] Though it has frequently been objected that it is hard to see how this assumption could be true (Van Fraassen 1989).

of those universals in the real world; what happens in the empirical world depends on and must be in accord with what relations hold among universals. This also ensures that laws are powerful—things happen because they say so. So *potency* is assured as well.

On *extent*, perhaps the issue is more open. Individual advocates may argue that laws govern all that happens. But that seems to be an add-on to the two assumptions that seem central to the account that, first, laws are relations between universals, and second, any instances of universals that figure in the laws must reflect in the appropriate way the relations among those universals. These do not by themselves imply that every feature that occurs in the world instances a universal that has such relations to others and hence the two do not seem to imply that everything that happens is in the purview of laws of nature. Even if one supposes that it makes no sense to think of features that do not fall under universals, there is still the issue of whether the associated universals all participate in the kinds of relations to one another that make for laws of nature.

Permissiveness may also be more open on the laws-as-relations-among-universals view than it seems at first sight. For there may be more relations among universals than just the one—labeled 'N'—that is the truth maker for the necessitation aspect of law claims. Some universals may be taller or more beautiful than others, which may be irrelevant to what happens in the world when these universals are instantiated. Even among world-guiding relations, necessitation may not be all there is. After all, the view presumably does not want to rule out that a probabilistic theory like quantum mechanics can be correct.

One way to allow for this is to keep only N and then suppose that the universal represented by the quantum state is N-related to a universal that we represent by a probability measure. Instantiation of this last seems troublesome though; moreover probability itself, as van Fraassen argues, may best be seen as a modal notion.[165] So, in keeping with the view that modalities reflect facts about universals and their relations, another idea for how to handle probabilistic laws is to assume there is another kind of modality beyond that responsible for necessity: 'probabilifies,' with various ways to develop this idea further. Key though is that if the universal corresponding to A probabilifies the universal corresponding to quantity Q in accord with Prob (Q = q), then instances of A will be associated with instances of values of Q in a pattern reflecting Prob (Q = q).

---

[165] Van Fraassen 1980.

This leads readily to admitting *permissiveness* of the kind we see in the capacities account of laws. Once more world-guiding relations are admitted than N, there seems no good reason to suppose that an even weaker modal notion than 'probabilifies' may obtain, one that constrains the values Q may take when A is instantiated to a given set but which dictates no particular pattern to them. One or another in the set must be instantiated but which on any occasion is mere hap, with not even a nice probability-looking pattern to emerge in the long run.

This may, at first sight, seem counter to the universals account of laws. After all, wasn't the point to find some location for necessity? We think not. The point is to find a location for *modality*. Universals are introduced in order to enable laws to do a number of jobs. They are supposed to support counterfactuals, to explain why things happen in the orderly way they do, to justify our inductive practices. All this may require modality but other modalities than necessity can do the jobs required. How is it on this view that the laws of nature *explain* that all Fs are Gs and justify our inductive practice of predicting that the next F we encounter will be G on the basis of past observations that Fs are Gs? It is because the universal associated with F is N-related to that associated with G. But it is not the N-ness of the relation that matters; it is rather the two-fold fact that this relation holds between the universals in Platonic heaven, and whatever world-guiding relations occur in Platonic heaven must be reflected in the behavior of their instances in the empirical world. Other kinds of patterns in the world could then be equally explained and supported by other relations between universals, for instance 'F probabilifies Q=q to degree p,' where the p values for Qs satisfy the probability calculus; or F φ-necessitates Q, which is reflected in the fact that Fs are always followed by some value or other of Q in φ.

4. Dispositions, à la Alexander Bird

So far we have mainly focused on Lewis's and Armstrong's accounts. Although they can both be seen as figureheads for rival camps concerning the laws of nature, Alexander Bird interestingly notes that the accounts have two theses in common.[166] They both take (i) laws of nature to be metaphysically contingent, and they both take (ii) properties to be categorical. Dispositional essentialism (DE) has emerged as an account of laws that

---
[166] Bird 2005, 2007.

explicitly rejects these two assumptions. First, according to DE, the laws of nature are metaphysically necessary, for reasons that we will see soon (though we shall have very little to say about what is supposed to be meant by 'metaphysically necessary'). Second, DE takes at least some—maybe all—natural properties to be essentially dispositional. We will briefly discuss in this section Alexander Bird's version of DE for a concrete illustration. Similar results with respect to contingency hold for many other versions, making appropriate adjustments.

First, Bird adopts the conditional analysis of dispositions (CA). Where D is a dispositional property, $S(D)$ is a stimulus property appropriate to it and $M(D)$ is its manifestation property, (CA) may be symbolized as follows:

(CA) $Dx \leftrightarrow (S(D)x \mathbin{\Box\!\!\rightarrow} M(D)x)$.

As Bird points out, (CA) does not merely provide an analysis of the concept D; instead, it characterizes the *nature* of the property D. Thus, as Bird says, (CA) is metaphysically necessary:

(CA$_\Box$) $\Box_M(Dx \leftrightarrow (S(D)x \mathbin{\Box\!\!\rightarrow} M(D)x))$.

Second, DE endorses the view that at least some fundamental properties are essentially dispositional. To say that a property P is essentially dispositional is to say that, necessarily—in the metaphysical sense—to instantiate P is to possess a disposition $D(P)$ to yield the appropriate manifestation in response to an appropriate stimulus:

(DE$_P$) $\Box_M(Px \rightarrow D(P)x)$

Here is how to explain "the truth of a generalisation on the basis of the dispositional essence of a property" (Bird 2007, 46):

1. $\Box_M(P(D)x \rightarrow (S(D)x \mathbin{\Box\!\!\rightarrow} M(D)x))$ from CA$_\Box$ and DE$_P$.
2. $P(D)x$ & $S(D)x$ assumption.
3. $M(D)x$ from 1 and 2.
4. $(P(D)x$ & $S(D)x) \rightarrow Mx$ from 2–3.

Since one can generalize over the unbound variable x, we get from 4

5. $\forall x\,((P(D)x$ & $S(D)x) \rightarrow M(D)x$.

Hence, a universal generalization follows from (CA$_\square$) and (DE$_P$). Furthermore, since both (CA$_\square$) and (DE$_P$) are metaphysically necessary, this generalization is metaphysically necessary as well. It looks then as if any laws underwritten by dispositional properties will be totally *reliable*, and on Bird's view it seems that these are all the laws there.

The problem with this, though, is that (CA) is often false, Bird notes, because of the existence of *finkish* dispositions and antidotes.[167] However, he argues, rather than being a disadvantage for dispositionalism, this is one of its virtues, since the falsity of (CA) allows the dispositionalist to account for ceteris paribus laws. We can just replace the left-to-right implication of (CA) by

(CA→ *) Dx → (S(D)x & *finks and antidotes to D are absent* $\square$→ M(D)x).

Now we deduce the following regularity:

∀x (*finks and antidotes to D are absent* → ((Dx & S(D)x) → M(D)x)).

This is how the dispositionalist can account for ceteris paribus laws—supposing that in all correct ceteris paribus laws, the conditions that are referred to in the ceteris paribus clause genuinely are either finks or antidotes to the disposition referred to. Conditioning on the absence of finks and antidotes gets built right into the laws themselves. *Reliability*, it seems, is thus restored, at least for ceteris paribus laws where all that is missing to render the ceteris paribus clause explicit is reference to finks or antidotes. Moreover, Bird also argues that there is a fundamental level of laws where no finks occur and where antidotes are very unlikely.[168] In that case, as above, *reliability* is assured by (CA), as already noted.

What then about *permissiveness*? It seems that where they speak—which seems to be whenever a dispositional property obtains and there are no

---

[167] "An object's disposition is finkish when the object loses the disposition after the occurrence of the stimulus but before the manifestation can occur and in such a way that consequently that manifestation does not occur" (Bird 2007, 25). See also Martin 1994 and Lewis 1997. Bird also points out that one cannot eliminate all counterexamples to (CA→) by excluding finks (Bird 2007, 27). "Let object x possess disposition D(S,M). At a time t it receives stimulus S and so in the normal course of things, at some later time t', x manifests M" (Bird 2007, 27). An antidote or mask to D(S,M) is something that "has the effect of breaking the causal chain leading to M, so that M does not in fact occur" when applied before t' (Bird 2007, 27) See Bird 1998.

[168] Bird 2007, 63.

finks or antidotes to it—DE laws allow only one outcome, the manifestation associated with that disposition. So DE laws seem impermissive. On the other hand, there seems to be nothing in the basic motivations for this account that implies that the manifestation must be limited to a single choice rather than a set of choices, with or without a probability over them. So impermissiveness seems an add-on for DE laws, just as it is for laws when taken as relations among universals or on the BSA.

Extent too seems to fare just the same as in the other two accounts so far surveyed, except perhaps limitations on extent are to be expected here, at least so far as the basics we have presented go. The issue is whether everything that happens is a manifestation of (some combination of) essentialist dispositions. Two ways they may not be are immediately evident. First, if not all properties are DE properties then DE laws that supervene on DE properties and their associated dispositions will not cover them.[169] Second, DE laws derived above are, as remarked, ceteris paribus laws, which cover only situations where no finks and antidotes obtain. What happens when these do? Or—more to the point—will finks and antidotes always be constituted by essentialist dispositional properties so that what happens when they obtain is then covered by the universal generalization that supervenes on the dispositions associated to those? If not, then DE laws won't cover everything that happens. So DE laws may well be limited in extent.

Recall though that Bird maintains that there is a level of fundamental dispositional properties that are not subject to finks and are seldom subject to antidotes. Does this imply that the correct set of laws covers all that happens? Supposing we substitute 'never' for 'seldom,' the answer is 'yes,' *if* a kind of total reductionism holds in which everything ultimately is covered by laws deriving from fundamental dispositional properties. But this kind of reductionism does not seem to follow from the basic motivating ideas of a DE account of laws. As with many of the other assumptions we have discussed, it is just an add-on.

The real issue for extent then depends on two things. First, are all properties, including those that feature in finks and antidotes, essentially dispositional? And second, are all complexes of properties—like: 'P(D) and the properties that characterize antidote A to P(D) and fink F to P(D)'—them-

---

[169] Some proponents of DE might, however, hold a mixed view according to which some fundamental properties are essentially dispositional and others are categorical, and so a DE law could connect a disposition with a categorical property. As a result, extent may be retained since laws won't supervene only on DE properties. Thanks to the editors for pointing this out.

selves essentially dispositional properties and hence properties that give rise to laws that can cover every case? Suppose the answer to both is 'yes.' Is that an add-on or rather a central part of the DE view? The answer here seems less clear than in many of the other cases we have considered and we won't take a view. But if the answer is yes and this is not deemed an add-on, then DE laws will be, by their nature, universal in extent.

What about *reliability*? Again let's look at what seems to be the hardest case—where the laws are deterministic, which is where much of the current philosophy of religion and metaphysics literature focuses. As we saw before, if the correct laws L are deterministic, then $\Box((P_0(L,P) \& L) \to P)$.

This is true also for Bird's account. But the main difference between Bird's view and the BSA is how they reply to Sehon's objection. If Sehon is right, then determinism should be compatible with 'IG' being logically possible. However, it should be noted that, in Sehon's argument, he reads boxes and diamonds as logical necessity and possibility. Thus, his reasoning is only relevant if the box of $\Box((P_0(L,P) \& L) \to P)$ is read as logical necessity. It will be clearer if we present his reasoning again. Let '$\Box_L$' and '$\Diamond_L$' respectively stand for logical necessity and possibility.

1. $\Box_L(IG \supset \Diamond(P_0(L,P) \& L \& \sim P))$ Premise.
2. $\Diamond_L IG$ Premise.
3. $\Diamond_L(P_0(L,P) \& L \& \sim P)$ From 1&2, assuming S4.
4. $\sim\Box_L((P_0(L,P) \& L) \supset P)$ From 3.

As we can see, 4 implies the contradictory of $\Box((P_0(L,P) \& L) \to P)$ if the box is read as logical necessity.

Now, if we take the initial or boundary conditions that feed into laws to be facts about the past, which is one typical choice for them, then Helen Beebee can help us think about the issue of logical necessity for 'Humean' views: 'For the Humean, the laws and the current facts determine the future facts in a *purely logical* way [our emphasis]: you can *deduce* future facts from current facts plus the laws. And this is just because *laws* are, in part, facts about the future.'[170] So, if the BSA is correct, then it should follow from determinism that $\Box_L((P_0(L,P) \& L) \to P)$, as indeed it does under the definition we adopted in Section 2. That is, according to the BSA, determinism is incompatible with 'IG' being logically possible *as possibility is characterized* by Sehon.

---

[170] Beebee 2000, 578.

On the other hand, if DE is correct, then it seems that determinism could be compatible with 'IG' being logically possible even *as characterized by Sehon*. This is so because the dispositionalist needs only one genuine notion of necessity that applies to issues about what happens in the world, which is metaphysical necessity (Bird 2007: 48). And metaphysical necessity is distinct from logical necessity. As a result, the box of $\Box((P_0(L,P) \& L) \to P)$ should be read as metaphysical necessity. Let '$\Box_M$' stand for metaphysical necessity. Now it is clear that

(L) $\sim\Box_L((P_0(L,P) \& L) \to P)$

and

(M) $\Box_M((P_0(L,P) \& L) \to P)$

are not *explicitly* contradictory. Someone might argue that (L) and (M) are implicitly contradictory. If logical possibility entails metaphysical possibility, then one gets the contradictory of (M); and then (L) and (M) are implicitly contradictory. Nevertheless, the dispositionalist has no motivation for accepting the premise that logical possibility entails metaphysical possibility. One might argue that we should expect a clear explanation of what metaphysical necessity is, since Bird's account relies on it. This might be correct. However, it is not our aim in this chapter to defend Bird's view but rather to show the consequences of his view for our discussion.

How though could DE reject the 'logically necessary' reading of the box in $((P_0(L,P) \& L) \to P)$ since we argued in Section 2 that that reading follows from the definition of determinism we adopt, which is not an unconventional one? It seems the trick would be to revise the definition of determinism so that it doesn't involve logical necessity either but only metaphysical necessity, thus:

> Laws L are *DE-deterministic* iff for any P that L covers and any $P_0(L,P)$ that is 'appropriate' input to L for P and any metaphysically possible worlds w, w' in which L, if w and w' agree on $P_0(L,P)$, they agree on whether P obtains.

This may indeed be a reasonable move for the DE advocate to make given the view that the only modalities that should play a role in these discussions about nature and its laws and possibilities are metaphysical ones.

The second point concerns the question of *free will*. Lewis's view gives motivation for rejecting one of the premises of the consequence argument, namely, the premise that the laws of nature are not up to anyone since laws of nature supervene on the facts and some facts may be up to agents. On the other hand, it seems that those sympathetic to DE should accept this premise because they should, it seems, accept not only rule alpha but the rule α':

(α') $\Box_M P \vdash \blacksquare P$.

To see why, for DE, the laws of nature are not up to us, then, remember that for the dispositionalist the laws of nature are metaphysically necessary. Consequently, L is also metaphysically necessary. That is,

1. $\Box_M L$.

Given rule α,' from 1 we can derive

2. $\blacksquare L$.

So, it does not really matter in this case how we interpret '$\blacksquare$.' If rule α' is valid, then proponents of DE should accept the premise that the laws of nature are not up to us.

5. Cartwright and Pemberton on Capacities and Arrangements

Following the language of Cartwright, we call the kinds of powers that Cartwright and Pemberton defend 'capacities.'[171] They do not use the term 'manifestation' since it would be ambiguous in their ontology. Capacities have a canonical way of acting, which is to be distinguished from what happens when they act. For each capacity, there is a prescribed set of ways in which it can act. When the capacity 'gravity' acts, it pulls, no matter what happens to the object on which it pulls. What actually happens depends on what other powers gravity cooperates with in the circumstances and what the arrangements are. When the arrangements are right, the activities of the powers give rise to regular behaviors, as in the orbits of the planets

---

[171] Cartwright 1989.

around the sun, or the browning of bread in a toaster, or the expulsion of magnetic fields in a superconductor. These kinds of arrangements are what Cartwright called 'nomological machines' and more recently are commonly called 'mechanisms.'[172] Whether there are contingencies in nature then depends on whether all arrangements that occur in nature are like nomological machines or mechanisms, where it has been supposed that a single kind of behavior is fixed, or whether the outcomes can sometimes be open, and if so, how this is possible on a capacities account of laws.

To begin with, we must be careful how we think of activities. The conditional account of dispositions and powers has it that for each disposition D there is a (possibly empty) set of stimuli S(D) and an outcome M(D) such that D obtains just in case if some s(D) ∈ S(D) occurs, then M(D), where *s* and *M* represent occurent features. Still in the grip of this account, we can slip into thinking of the activity as an occurent feature like s(D) and M(D). As argued in chapter 2, this makes for puzzles when powers act in consort. The outcomes of each power separately then seem to be pictured as 'really there' as outcomes, though it seems they are often invisible. The visible, or occurent, outcome is the result of the powers acting jointly.

The model here is bricks in a wall (or, as in chapter 2, the two halves of a homogeneous fused-quartz sphere). Each brick is really there and so too is the wall. Some real cases can be fitted into this model, for instance where the outcomes can be represented with numbers that simply add up. We have the power to put $10 into the piggybank and you do too. When we all act, the total outcome is $20 sitting there in the piggybank, $20 that is genuinely made up of our $10 and your $10. Perhaps it is not even too much of a stretch to fit forces into this model. When the gravitational capacity associated with mass M acts, it produces a force $GMm/\mathbf{r}^2$ on another mass m located $\mathbf{r}$ from it; the Coulombic capacity associated with charge Q produces a force $\epsilon Qq/\mathbf{r}^2$ on a charge q located $\mathbf{r}$ from it. When both act together, they add vectorially. Perhaps we could without too much stretch say that all three forces are really there and in the same sense, as with the bricks and the wall.

But, as argued in chapter 2, this is a poor model for other capacities acting in consort, like the capacities associated with parts of a circuit—conductors, resistors, impedances—producing a total current. Nature may assign each capacity its own role, a role that it has qua the capacity that it is; and nature may—or may not—have a system to fix what happens when capacities act

---

[172] Cartwright 1989.

in consort in given circumstances. But nature need not do this via a simple model where each capacity separately produces its own canonical effect and what results overall just is all these separate effects piled up together.

As noted in chapter 2, because they want to avoid any suggestion of this picture, Cartwright and Pemberton have abandoned their former language of capacities, contributions, and rules of combination that determine outcomes in favor of capacities, exercisings or actings, and outcomes, following Peter Machamer, Lindley Darden, and Carl Craver's emphasis on activities.[173] A capacity acts in a canonical way, which is represented in various different ways in scientific theories in different domains, and when capacities act in consort in a particular arrangement, an outcome occurs. For Cartwright-Pemberton capacities, there is indeed a difference between the obtaining of a power and its exercise, as there should be, in defense against Hume, who couldn't keep these two distinct things in his ontology. But that does not make the exercising yet another occurent feature of the same kind as the resultant outcome.

There is a second good reason for avoiding the language of contributions and how they combine. That makes it sound as if the capacity could act outside of any situation and the contribution is just what happens then. But capacities always act in some situation or other. We must not confuse the abstract label we use for a capacity, which helps us to figure out what will happen in various real situations, with a description of what it does in some strange situation-less Platonic heaven. Perhaps we are sometimes led into this conflation by our conceptual model of the ideal experiment in which the capacity acts 'entirely on its own,' from which we sometimes read some canonical expression that we then use in making predictions about other circumstances, in accord with rules we have worked out about how to do this. But it is important to keep in mind that these idealized models picture concrete arrangements located in space and time, albeit ones that might never really occur.

We emphasize this to underline the lesson of chapters 2, 3, and 7: Arrangements matter. We may imagine two masses, M and m, located close together, m at **r** away from M, far away from anything else and also devoid of any other features, like charge, that are associated with a capacity to produce forces. Mass m would then experience a force very near to GMm/r^2, which is just the canonical description we give of the capacity of gravitational attraction in order to compute by our rule of vector addition the

---

[173] Machamer et al. 2000.

force exerted on a massive object in more complex arrangements. That however is an arrangement, albeit one very special one that we have discovered gives us a convenient way to represent the capacity of gravity for use in studying other arrangements. It takes a combination of a capacity with its peculiar nature (that in the case of gravitational attraction we represent by GMm/$\mathbf{r}^2$) *and* a given arrangement (like two objects both charged and massive being located close together and far away from all other objects) to fix what happens. This becomes important when we try to identify sources of contingency.

What kinds of general facts are there that might get labeled 'laws of nature' on a capacities account? (Note that following all the objections in earlier chapters to the idea that Nature operates 'by law', it would be better to us a more neutral term, like 'principle'. Here we stick with 'law' since we think the points we make here can be useful even for those who do not buy that Nature is an artful modeler.) Three, it seems. First, what the nature of a power is. It is in the nature of the power of gravity to attract with a fixed strength. We represent this with the concept 'the force of gravity' and represent the strength of gravity associated with a body of mass M on m located $\mathbf{r}$ away by *GM/$\mathbf{r}^2$*. Second, depending on one's metaphysics of properties, laws should include facts either about what powers co-occur or what properties bring with them what powers. For example, mass brings the power of gravity with it; or, if properties are just to be collections of powers, we could label as a law of nature the general fact that the power to attract gravitationally comes with the power to resist acceleration by a force. Third, laws should include what general facts there may be[174] about what happens when powers act, either singly or in consort, in various arrangements. For instance (supposing that resultant forces and not just motions are really there), when the power of gravity vested in M acts in a situation where m is located $\mathbf{r}$ away and no other sources of force on m are present, then M exerts a force GMm/$\mathbf{r}^2$ on m. Or, in a situation where two powers we represent as forces act together on a body at a given point, then the body experiences at that point a force which is given by the vector sum of the canonical representations of the two powers.

With this in hand, we can look to sources of contingency. Begin with *permissiveness*. On a capacity account of laws, *permissiveness* can arise along three axes: in the nature of the capacities themselves; in the rules of com-

---

[174] Recall the arguments in chapter 1 that we should not expect to find enough of these to cover the vast majority of things that happen in world.

bination when capacities act together; and in the effects of arrangement on what happens, though the last two will merge except in special cases.

The nature of a capacity. In line with the discussion in chapter 2, we can think of capacities as having three different possible modes of acting. First, there is one and only one mode of action for the capacity. No *permissiveness* here. Second, there is a set of available ways of acting and a probability over these. The capacity must act in accord with these probabilities. Versions of the propensity theory of quantum probabilities fit here. Third, the capacity may have an available set of modes of acting but no constraints on how often it acts in which ways even in the long run. Both these last two can lead to contingency about what happens when the capacity acts in specific arrangements.

Rules of combination. The familiar rule of vector addition fixes a single force that results in arrangements where two sources of force act together. But we can imagine *permissive* rules that allow a range of outcomes, either with or without a probability over them. Then what results would be contingent in the *permissiveness* sense.

The effects of the arrangement. Of course the effects of the arrangement are already there in the rules of combination. But we hive this off as a different source of contingency to deal with cases where the rules of combination do not cover all aspects of a situation that are relevant to what happens. We are thinking here of cases where experience shows that a given arrangement gives rise to some constraints or other on joint outcomes but there are no known rules of combination to explain this.[175] There is a general tendency in cases like this to think that the description of the situation is not detailed enough; when the details are filled in appropriately, there will be a general rule of combination to cover the case. That may—or may not—be so. The point is that there is nothing in the very notion of laws as facts about capacities and how they act in arrangements that precludes this source of contingency.

Consider *extent* next. One may argue, as some do, that there is nothing but powers and their activities, in which case everything that happens must be the result of this. But just as with the other views of laws, this is an add-on to the basic account of what laws are for a capacities account and probably for most other powers accounts. Nothing about powers in themselves says they must rule everywhere and everything.

---

[175] One might argue that where outcomes are constrained, there must be a rule of combination, albeit a very local one. That's fine. We include this as a separate category to ensure attention is not focused entirely on well-established general rules of combination.

As to *reliability*, the situation seems different. There seems no space in the capacity account to allow that things could happen within the domain of laws about capacities and about their joint outcomes that the powers-cum-arrangements do not allow. There seems to be no wiggle room on this account to allow that the laws of nature (which recall are about the natures of powers, what properties correlate with them, and how they are to act in various arrangements) could be as they are and yet for something about which they speak to occur contrary to what they say. Or at least we have not identified any such wiggle room.

Free will. This does not imply however that agents could not have acted otherwise than as they did. After all, the laws could be *permissive*. Or the actions of agents could be outside their domain. If though we insist on the analogue of determinism and universal domain for capacities, then it seems that on a capacities account an agent could not, consistent with those being the correct laws, have done otherwise than what she did do.

There is an intermediate position even here. The laws for agents could be *permissive* consistent with those for non-agents being *impermissive* so long as only non-agents are involved. In that case, when agents and non-agents act together in certain arrangements, multiple outcomes could be available, including both, for example, that the agent raises her hand and that she does not. There will of course be trouble for this last alternative if it turns out that agents are just special arrangements of non-agents.

6. Conclusion and an Observation

The observation is about our discussion of *free will*. For many, what we have discussed under this label is not only very cursory but also has little, even nothing, to do with free will because we have not touched on the 'will' part. Perhaps an agent could do differently from what she does but (and now the very form of this question itself is part of the serious enquiry) something like: 'Can she do so because she wills it?' Or, 'Can she cause it to happen?' After all, establishing that A's actions could have been otherwise is a long way from showing that A is the author of her actions. Conversely, one venerable Christian tradition[176] along with some modern libertarian thought[177] argues that being the author of one's actions does not imply

---
[176] Augustine 1993.
[177] Frankfurt 1969 and Mawson 2011.

that one could have done otherwise. Perhaps authorship is where attention should be in the contemporary debate anyway and not, as much seems to be, on the compatibility of free will with determinism since it has been a long time since our best science has supposed that the laws of nature are all deterministic.

At least we hope to have clarified that even if laws govern and in some sense 'make things happen,' there is nothing in the very nature of law in any of the senses surveyed that implies that things couldn't happen other than the way they do consistent with the laws staying the same, nor even that probabilities need be fixed. Laws may be universal in *extent* and yet totally *impermissive*, and one may—or may not—have good independent arguments for these add-ons; but in all senses of 'laws' surveyed that is just what these are: add-ons.

Conclusion: There are two surprises from this work, counter to our starting hypotheses. First, there are a number of different forms of contingency that are worth distinguishing and, contrary to initial expectations, contingency is no more readily admissible in any of these senses on a capacities (i.e. Cartwright and Pemberton powers) account of laws than on those that take laws as strong unifying regularities (BSA), as relations among universals, or as facts about dispositions of the Alexander Bird style (or as the metaphysically necessary facts about regularities that follow from these). All these equally can, but need not, allow laws to be both *permissive* and limited in *extent*.

The second surprise is *reliability*. We use this label to pick out a view easy to say in plain English but hard to make precise, that the laws of nature may remain the laws they are, the correct laws, and yet be 'violated' or broken in their own domain. Violation—*unreliability* in our terms—fares badly on all accounts, except surprisingly, a David Lewis style best systems account, supposing we are willing to make an adjustment either to the notion of violation or to the BSA itself, where the adjustments rely heavily on a notion of 'almost true.' Under the soft determinism wiggle, though it is dressed up in the possibly impressive-looking quasi-formal language of possible worlds, the final verdict is that the correct laws are never violated in the strong sense. If something seemingly untoward happens (e.g. God intervenes), this can be a violation of some 'almost true' laws that prohibit it but not of the correct laws. The laws-as-templates wiggle gives up on the precise truth of the correct law claims: the regular associations that constitute the laws do not really hold; they only 'almost' hold.

This is surprising in the context of much current discussion of 'compatibilism' in metaphysics—Is an interventionist God/free will compatible with deterministic law?—which seems to suppose the BSA. If we are right that *reliability* is unavoidable on the other accounts but could perhaps fail on the BSA, then this literature is focused on the easiest case for avoiding reliability.[178]

---

[178] Thanks to the editors of the volume *Laws of Nature* in which this chapter was first published for helpful comments and thanks to Keith Ward for pressing issues of the extent of permissiveness. Cartwright's research for this was in part supported by the Templeton-funded LSE/UCSD project, *God's Order, Man's Order and the Order of Nature* and in part by the Durham project *Knowledge for Use (K4U)*, which has received funding from the European Research Council (ERC) under the European Union's Horizon 2020 research and innovation program (grant agreement No 667526 K4U). The content reflects only the author's view and the ERC is not responsible for any use that may be made of the information it contains. Merlussi's research for this was supported by the CAPES Foundation.

7

The Natural and the Moral Order: What's to Blame?

"You cannot derive ought from is." This is a lesson that has been taught generation after generation for centuries. Yet it is regularly ignored. Lorraine Daston has a story that helps make sense of this. When we want to think about what is right, to understand what constitutes a good society or a good life or a good set of actions—or to figure out how to achieve these—we need a model of order; and our most readily available, and perhaps only suitable, model is that of the order of nature. The natural order becomes our model for the moral order.

I want to develop this story by exploring some examples from an area I have been working in recently, jointly with philosopher of social science Eleonora Montuschi and Eileen Munro, author of the UK Government's 2011 *Munro Review of Child Protection*: child welfare. Here we see that ideas about the moral and the natural order are inextricably intertwined and that different understandings of the natural order flow across to the moral. The central conduit between the two are linked views about causality and responsibility. So, although I illustrate with the child welfare cases, the lessons should apply far more broadly.

When it comes to thinking about causality, there is a venerable tradition in philosophy that pictures the modeling relation the other way around: from the moral order to the natural. This tradition is rooted in the idea that causation, though a relation of central importance to our ability to predict and control, is not a genuine sui generis relation in the natural world. What then is it? There are, first off, various versions of the currently popular manipulation theory of causality, that causes are things we can manipulate to produce results. The canonical version of a second account of what it is is due to the legal philosophers H.L.A. Hart and Tony Honoré, who single out from the net of events in the past of an outcome, that the cause is the event that is contrary to the norm, where very often this will be a legal, moral or social norm. The Hart and Honoré account will play a role in my discussion but it is not my central focus for I am looking to cases where different ideas about how causes operate in the natural order support different moral and social norms.

Let us begin with a case. In 2004 in the London Borough of Haringey, seventeen-month-old Peter Connelly was found dead in his crib. The child had suffered fractured ribs and a broken back after months of abuse at home. His mother, her partner and a lodger were jailed for his death. Peter had been seen by health and social services professionals from Haringey Council sixty times in the eight months before he died. In consequence, blame was heaped on the Director of Haringey Children's Services, Sharon Shoesmith. For instance, the Minister of Education Ed Balls sacked Shoesmith with immediate effect in a live press conference on television; and both the news media and the public were openly hostile to Shoesmith. She even received death threats in the mail for her supposed role in Peter Connelly's death.

There seem to be two rationales for this. One is the desire for prevention; the other, outrage and the need to punish. A BBC news interviewer represented the first when he urged: If nobody accepts the blame, "how can we stop it happening again?"[179] Eileen Munro gives a good sense of the second when she says: "When society is shocked and outraged by a child's terrible tale of suffering, there seems a basic human desire to find a culprit, someone to bear the guilt for the disaster and to be the target of feelings of rage and frustration."[180]

Shoesmith defended herself and her Services: "We should not be put into blame"; it does not produce "anything productive" and obscures "the bigger picture."[181] If not that, then what *should* we do? Munro offers an alternative, though not incompatible, perspective when she claims that one should see "child protection as a systems problem."[182]

These two moral perspectives mirror two different models of the production of outcomes in the natural order. The first focuses on causal pro-

---

[179] "Shoesmith: 'I don't do blame'."
[180] Munro 2005, 378.
[181] "Shoesmith: 'I don't do blame'."
[182] Munro 2005, 375.

cesses, or causal chains; the second on what I have called "nomological machines" and subsequent work, primarily in the philosophy of biology, labels "mechanisms."

Causal processes first. A causal process or causal chain is a series of happenings, each one of which produces the next, one after the other, until at last the outcome in view is achieved. Studying these processes is the meat and potatoes of much of modern scientific endeavor, from process tracing in biomedical science and toxicology to a vast variety of statistical comparative methods, including the rampant use of randomized controlled trials in medicine and increasingly in social science, that aim to show *that* such a process has occurred, albeit without tracing out its steps. And when it comes to policy, from education to crime to early childhood intervention or aging, there is now, as I noted in chapter 3, a huge evaluation industry whose job is not just to measure outcomes to determine whether a policy has been followed by the desired outcomes but rather to show whether the policy was responsible for those outcomes—whether the policy and the outcome were connected by an appropriate causal process.

This kind of evaluation methodology is at the heart of the blame attribution we observe in cases like that of Peter Connelly. As Munro describes, when a tragedy like the death of Peter Connelly occurs, "The standard response is to hold an inquiry, looking in detail at the case and trying to get a picture of the causal sequence of events that ended in the child's death. ... We are tracing a chain of events back in time to understand how it happened...."[183] Here the moral and natural order dissolve into one another. Where does the backwards tracing stop? As Munro points out, the "events that bring the investigation to a halt usually take the form of human error."[184]

Munro also notes a peculiar feature of these child welfare cases, reflected in the death threats that Sharon Shoesmith received, which connects them with the Hart and Honoré account of causation: "Unlike the police investigation, which focuses on the perpetrators of the homicide, these inquiries focus primarily on how the professionals acted, judging them against the formal procedures for working with families and principles of good practice."[185] That is, they look for deviations from the norms of professional behavior: "Practitioners did not comply with procedures or lapsed from accepted standards of good practice."[186]

---

[183] Munro 2005, 377.
[184] Munro 2005, 378.
[185] Munro 2005, 377.
[186] Munro 2005, 377–78.

But as a UK Department of Health pamphlet explains,

> There are two ways of viewing human error: the person-centred approach and the system approach. The [person-centred] . . . approach focuses on the psychological precursors of error, such as inattention, forgetfulness and carelessness. Its associated countermeasures are aimed at individuals rather than situations and these invariably fall within the "control" paradigm of management. Such controls include disciplinary measures, writing more procedures to guide individual behaviour, or blaming, naming and shaming.[187]

And this is just what we saw in the case of Sharon Shoesmith with Ed Balls and the BBC interviewer.

The Department of Health itself note the parallels in the moral and natural order involved:

> Aside from treating errors as moral issues, [the person-centred approach] isolates unsafe acts from their context, thus making it very hard to uncover and eliminate recurrent error traps within the system.
>
> The system approach, in contrast, takes a holistic stance on the issues of failure. It recognises that many of the problems facing organisations are complex, ill-defined and result from the interaction of a number of factors.[188]

So, what's a system? Systems—or "mechanisms"—are our second model of how outcomes are produced in the natural order. This model admits causal processes but the processes are not basic. They are in need of deeper explanation. Recall the discussion of the context-centered approach in chapter 3. What causal processes can happen and what ones will happen regularly depend on an underlying mechanism that gives rise to them. A mechanism is composed of a number of different parts interacting in some kind of arrangement that makes it explicable why some kinds of causal processes will occur and others will be precluded. A toaster is a mechanism. The structure of the toaster—its parts and the way they are arranged and interact—explains why it is possible to produce toast by plugging it in and pressing on the lever.

But mechanisms need not be mechanical in any sense and indeed, as I mentioned, much of the philosophical work on them recently has been

---
[187] UK Department of Health 2000, 20.
[188] UK Department of Health 2000, 21.

done in studying biology. For instance, when we investigate the firing of neurons, we discover that the receipt of neurotransmitter particles produces a potential difference across the wall at one end of the neuron which causes the movement of this potential difference to move along the neuron. It's no accident that this process happens, nor that it happens in neurons and not in other places. The scientists investigating this process discovered sodium selective pores in the lining of the neuron wall which open and close to control the movement of a cloud of sodium ions into and out of the neuron, thus supporting the propagation of a potential difference along the neuron. They were learning what the relevant parts of the "mechanism" are and how the arrangement and interactions of these parts allow the causal process under study to occur.

Nor need mechanisms be relatively sturdy, as the toaster is; they can be fragile and easy to break, like a fragile peace. Nor need they be static. They can be dynamic, they can change and they can evolve. They can have porous boundaries and it may be ill-defined what is in and what is out of the mechanism at any time or whether we continue to see the same mechanism across changes in parts and their interactions, or a different one. What matters is that it is the way some parts are arranged and interact that makes possible and explains the causal processes that happen and that are likely or unlikely to happen.

Social systems, made up of interacting individuals and institutions with their norms, conventions and habits—these too are mechanisms: mechanisms that afford causal processes. Some support desirable causal processes, or undesirable; other make it difficult for these processes to occur. And with this model too, the natural and the moral order dissolve into one another. This is vividly illustrated in the US National Academy of Sciences' *To Err Is Human: Building a Safer Health System*:

> The title of this report encapsulates its purpose. Human beings, in all lines of work, make errors. Errors can be prevented by designing systems that make it hard for people to do the wrong thing and easy for people to do the right thing. Cars are designed so that drivers cannot start them while in reverse because that prevents accidents. Work schedules for pilots are designed so they don't fly too many consecutive hours without rest because alertness and performance are compromised.[189]

---

[189] Kohn, Corrigan, and Donaldson 2000, ix.

The NAS report urges: "The focus must shift from blaming individuals for past errors to a focus on preventing future errors by designing safety into the system."[190]

From the systems point of view, the causal process model is the wrong model, not just for the natural order, because it focuses only on surface phenomena and misses out on explanatory depth, but for the moral order. For the kinds of preventative measures the causal process model leads to—recall the UK Department of Health examples: disciplinary actions, writing more procedures to guide individual behavior, or blaming, naming and shaming—these measures are generally unlikely to stop these kinds of sequences from occurring.

Whether or not the natural order is our most plausible or most available model for moral order, at least in these cases of causation and responsibility the two cannot be easily pried apart.

---

[190] Kohn, Corrigan, and Donaldson 2000, 5.

References

American Psychological Association. 2018. "Journals in Assessment, Evaluation, Measurement, Psychometrics and Statistics" [online]. Available at: http://www.apadivisions.org/division-5/resources/journals.aspx [Accessed March 2018].

Anscombe, G.E.M. 1971. *Causality and Determination: An Inaugural Lecture.* London: Cambridge University Press.

Armstrong, D. 1983. *What Is a Law of Nature?* Cambridge: Cambridge University Press.

Augustine. 1993 *On the Free Choice of the Will.* Trans. Thomas Williams. Indianapolis: Hackett Publishing.

Austin, J. L. 1956–1957. "A Plea for Excuses." *Proceedings of the Aristotelian Society* 57: 1–30.

Banerjee, A.V., and E. Duflo. 2011. *Poor Economics: A Radical Rethinking of the Way to Fight Global Poverty.* New York: Public Affairs.

Beebee, H. 2000. "The Nongoverning Conception of Laws of Nature." *Philosophy and Phenomenological Research* 61: 571–94.

Bird, A. 1998. "Dispositions and Antidotes." *Philosophical Quarterly* 48: 227–34.

———. 2005. "The Dispositionalist Conception of Laws." *Foundations of Science* 10: 353–70.

———. 2007. *Nature's Metaphysics: Laws and Properties.* Oxford: Oxford University Press.

Bird, A. 2010. "Eliminative Abduction—Examples from Medicine." *Studies in History and Philosophy of Science* (41): 345–52.

Blümle, A., J. J. Meerpohl, G. Rücker, G. Antes, M. Schumacher, and E. von Elm. 2011. "Reporting of Eligibility Criteria of Randomised Trials: Cohort Study Comparing Trial Protocols with Subsequent Articles. *BMJ* 342: d1828.

The British Horological Institute. 2008. *The Practical Lubrication of Watches and Clocks.* Available at: https://www.yumpu.com/en/document/view/39254836/

the-practical-lubrication-of-watches-and-clocks-british- [Accessed February 2018].

Cartwright, N. 1979. "Causal Laws and Effective Strategies." *Nous* 13(4): 419–37.

———. 1983. *How the Laws of Physics Lie*. Oxford: Clarendon Press.

———. 1989. *Nature's Capacities and Their Measurement*. Abingdon: Clarendon Press.

———. 1998. "How Theories Relate: Takeovers or Partnerships?" *Philosophia Naturalis* 35:23–34.

———. 1999. *The Dappled World: A Study of the Boundaries of Science*. Cambridge: Cambridge University Press.

———. 2000. "Against the Completability of Science." In *The Proper Ambition of Science.*, ed. J. Wolff and M.W.F. Stone. New York: Routledge.

———. 2007. *Hunting Causes and Using Them: Approaches in Philosophy and Economics*. Cambridge: Cambridge University Press.

———. 2009. "Causal Laws, Policy Predictions and the Need for Genuine Powers." In *Dispositions and Causes,* ed T. Handfield. Oxford: Oxford University Press.

———. 2010. "Natural Laws and the Closure of Physics." In *Visions of Discovery: New Light on Physics, Cosmology and Consciousness,* ed. R. Y. Chiao, M. L. Cohen, A. J. Leggett, W. D. Phillips, and C. L. Harper, 612–22. Cambridge: Cambridge University Press.

———. 2013a. "Evidence, Argument and Prediction." In *EPSA11 Perspectives and Foundational Problems in Philosophy of Science, The European Philosophy of Science Association Proceedings 2*, ed. V. Karakostas and D. Dieks. Cham, Switzerland: Springer International Publishing.

———. 2013b. *Evidence: For Policy and Wheresoever Rigor is a Must*. London: LSE.

Cartwright, N., J. Cat, L. Fleck, and T. E. Uebel. 1996. *Otto Neurath: Philosophy Between Science and Politics*. Cambridge: Cambridge University Press.

Cartwright, N., and J. Hardie. 2012. *Evidence-Based Policy: A Practical Guide to Doing It Better*. New York: Oxford University Press.

Cartwright, N., and J. M. Pemberton. 2013. "Aristotelian Powers: Without Them What Would Modern Science Do?" In *Powers and Capacities in Philosophy: The New Aristotelianism*, ed. J. Greco and R. Groff, 93–112. New York: Routledge.

Cartwright, N., and K. Ward, eds. 2016. *Rethinking Order: After the Laws of Nature*. London: Bloomsbury.

Cartwright, N., and P. Merlussi. 2018. "Are Laws of Nature Consistent with Contingency?" In *Laws of Nature*, ed. W. Ott and L. Patto, 221–44. Oxford: Oxford University Press. Also as a Working Paper at the Centre for Humanities

Engaging Science and Society (CHESS), Durham. Available at: http://dro.dur.ac.uk/20088/1/20088.pdf?DDD24+cmdm84+dul4eg [Accessed March 2018].

Cartwright, N., S. Wieten, and J. Pemberton. 2018. "Mechanisms, Ceteris Paribus Laws and Covering-law Explanation." [Working paper]. Centre for Humanities Engaging Science and Society (CHESS), Durham. Available at: https://www.dur.ac.uk/resources/chess/K4U_BLANKWP_2018_04.pdf [Accessed January 2019].

Chang, H. 2004. *Inventing Temperature: Measurement and Scientific Progress*. New York: Oxford University Press.

———. 2017. "Pragmatist Coherence as the Source of Truth and Reality." *Proceedings of the Aristotelian Society* 117(2): 103–22.

———. Forthcoming. *Realism for Realistic People: A New Pragmatist Philosophy of Science*. Cambridge: Cambridge University Press.

Cohen, J., and C. Callender. 2009. "A Better Best System Account of Lawhood." *Philosophical Studies* 145: 1–34.

Deaton, A. 2012. "Searching for Answers Using RTCs?" *Debates in Development: The Search for Answers* [Conference Paper], Princeton University.

Deaton, A., and N. Cartwright. 2017. "Understanding and Misunderstanding Randomized Controlled Trials." *Social Science and Medicine* 210: 2–21.

Dicks, L.V., J. E. Ashpole, J. Dänhardt, K. James, A. Jönsson, N. Randall, D. A. Showler, R. K. Smith, S. Turpin, D. R. Williams, and W. J. Sutherland. 2017. "Farmland Conservation." In *What Works in Conservation 2017*, ed. W. J. Sutherland, L. V. Dicks, and R. K. Smith. Cambridge: Open Book Publishers.

Dretske, F. I. 1977. "Laws of Nature." *Philosophy of Science* 44 (2): 248–68.

Duhem, Pierre. 1991.*The Aim and Structure of Physical Theory*. [1906]. Reprint. Princeton: Princeton University Press.

Earman, J. 1978. "The Universality of Laws." *Philosophy of Science* 45 (2): 173–81.

Einstein, A., and L. Infeld. 1938. *The Evolution of Physics*. Cambridge University Press: Cambridge.

Elgin, C. 2012. "Understanding's Tethers." In *Epistemology: Contexts, Values, Disagreement: Proceedings of the 34th International Ludwig Wittgenstein Symposium, Kirchberg am Wechsel, Austria 2011*, ed. Christoph Jäger and Winfried Löffler, 131–46. Berlin: De Gruyter.

Epstein, P. 1924. "On the Resistance Experienced by Spheres in their Motion through Gases." *Physics Review* 23: 710–33.

Fischer, F. 2018. "Laws of Nature as Dispositions." PhD diss., Rheinische Friedrich-Wilhelms-Universität, Bonn.

Frankfurt, H. G. 1969. "Alternate Possibilities and Moral Responsibility." *Journal of Philosophy* 66: 828–39.

Friend, T. 2016. "Laws Are Conditionals." *European Journal for Philosophy of Science* 6(1): 123–44.

Frisch, M. 2012. "No Place for Causes? Causal Skepticism in Physics." *European Journal for Philosophy of Science* 2.3: 313–36.

Gigerenzer, G., P. M. Todd, and the ABC Research Group. 1999. *Simple Heuristics that Make Us Smart*. New York: Oxford University Press.

Ginet, C. 1983. "In Defence of Incompatibilism." *Philosophical Studies* 44: 391–400.

Gough, D., S. Oliver, and J. Thomas. 2013. *Learning from Research: Systematic Reviews for Informing Policy Decisions: A Quick Guide*. A paper for the Alliance for Useful Evidence. London: Nesta.

Harré, R., and E. h. Madden. 1975. *Causal Powers*. Blackwell: Oxford.

Heil, J. 2005. "Dispositions." *Synthese* 144(3): 343–56.

Hendry, R. F. 2017. "Molecular Structure within Quantum Mechanics" [email]. Personal communication, 27 January 2017.

Humphreys, M. 2015. "What Has Been Learned from the Deworming Replications: A Nonpartisan View" [online]. Available at: http://www.columbia.edu/%7Emh2245/w/worms.html [Accessed March 2018].

Jones, O. 2014. "Can This HIV Drug Help to End 30 Years of Blighted Lives? *The Guardian* [online]. Available at: https://www.theguardian.com/commentisfree/2014/sep/29/new-hiv-drug-truvada-gay-men-us-nhs [Accessed February 2018].

Klassen, S. 2009. "Identifying and Addressing Student Difficulties with the Millikan Oil Drop Experiment." *Science and Education* 18:593–607.

Kohn, L., J. Corrigan, and M. Donaldson, eds. 2000. *To Err Is Human: Building a Safer Health System*. Washington, D.C.: National Academy Press.

Kuhn, T. 1970. *The Structure of Scientific Revolutions*. Chicago and London: University of Chicago Press.

Lakatos, I., and A. Musgrave, eds. 1972. *Criticism and the Growth of Knowledge: Proceedings of the International Colloquium in the Philosophy of Science, London, 1965*. Cambridge: Cambridge University Press.

Lewis, D. 1973. *Counterfactuals*. Cambridge: Harvard University Press.

———. 1979. "Counterfactual Dependence and Time's Arrow." *Noûs* 13: 455–76.

———. 1981. "Are We Free to Break the Laws?" *Theoria* 47: 113–21.

———. 1983. "New Work for a Theory of Universals." *Australasian Journal of Philosophy* 61: 343–77.

———. 1994. "Humean Supervenience Debugged." *Mind* 103 (412): 473–90.

———. 1997. "Finkish Dispositions." *Philosophical Quarterly* 47: 143–58.

Loewer, B. 1996. "Humean Supervenience." *Philosophical Topics* 24(1): 101–27.

Longino, H. E. 2013. *Studying Human Behavior: How Scientists Investigate Aggression and Sexuality.* Chicago: University of Chicago Press.

Machamer, P., L. Darden, and C. F. Craver. 2000. Thinking about Mechanisms. *Philosophy of Science* 67(1): 1–25.

Mackie, J. L. 1965. "Causes and Conditions." *American Philosophical Quarterly* 12: 245–65.

———. 1974. *The Cement of the Universe.* Oxford: Clarendon Press.

Marcus, R. B. 1975-6. "Dispensing with Possibilia." *Proceedings and Addresses of the American Philosophical Association, 'Possibilia and Possible Worlds'* 49: 39–51.

Marmodoro, A. 2018. "Potentiality in Aristotle's Metaphysics." In *The Handbook of Potentiality,* ed. K. Engelhard and M. Quante. Netherlands: Springer.

Martin, C. B. 1994. "Dispositions and Conditionals." *Philosophical Quarterly* 44: 1–8.

Mawson, T. J. 2011. *Free Will: A Guide for the Perplexed.* New York: Continuum Press.

McKitrick, J. 2010. Manifestations as Effects. In *The Metaphysics of Powers: Their Grounding and their Manifestations,* ed. A. Mormodoro, 73–83. Routledge: New York.

Miguel, E., and M. Kramer. 2004. "Worms: Identifying Impacts on Education and Health in the Presence of Treatment Externalities." *Econometrica* 72: 159–217.

Mill, J. S. 1948. *Essays on some Unsettled Questions of Political Economy* [1830]. London School of Economics and Political Science: London.

Millikan, R. A. 1911. "The Isolation of an Ion, a Precision Measurement of Its Charge, and the Correction of Stokes's Law." *Physics Review* 32: 349–97.

———. 1913. "On the Elementary Electrical Charge and the Avogadro Constant." *Physics Review* 11(2): 109–43.

Morgan, M. S. 2009. "Traveling Facts." In *How Well Do Facts Travel?: The Dissemination of Reliable Knowledge,* ed. Mary S. Morgan and Peter Howlett, 3–42. Cambridge: Cambridge University Press.

Mumford, S., and R. L. Anjum. 2011. *Getting Causes from Powers.* Oxford: Oxford University Press.

Munro, E. 2005. "Improving Practice: Child Protection as a Systems Problem." *Children and Youth Services Review* 27.

NAM Publications. 2018. "How effective is PrEP?" [online]. Available at: http://www.aidsmap.com/How-effective-is-PrEP/page/2983351/ [Accessed February 2018].

Norton, J. 2014. "A Material Defense of Inductive Inference" [manuscript]. Available at: https://www.pitt.edu/~jdnorton/papers/Skepticism_Induction.pdf [Accessed February 2018].

Oxford Living Dictionaries. 2018. *Wissenschaft*. Available at: https://en.oxforddictionaries.com/definition/wissenschaft [Accessed February 2018].

Pissarides, C. 2007. "Unemployment and Hours of Work: The North Atlantic Divide Revisited." *International Economic Review* 48(1): 1–36.

Prior, E. 1985. *Dispositions*. Aberdeen: Aberdeen University Press.

Pruss, A. 2013. "Incompatibilism Proved." *Canadian Journal of Philosophy* 43 (4): 430–37.

Quine, W. V. 1948. "On What There Is." *Review of Metaphysics* 2(5): 21–38.

Ramsey, F. 1978. *Foundations*. London: Routledge and Kegan Paul.

Reichenbach, H. 1947. *Elements of Symbolic Logic*. New York: The Macmillan Company.

Reiss, J. 2015. *Causation, Evidence, and Inference*. New York: Routledge.

Roberts, J. T. 2008. *The Law-Governed Universe*. Oxford: Oxford University Press.

San Francisco Health Network. 2016. "Pre-Exposure Prophylaxis (PrEP) Management Guidelines" [online]. Available at: https://hiv.ucsf.edu/docs/prep-guide_june2016-2.pdf [Accessed February 2018].

Scheibe, E. 1991. "Substances, Physical Systems, and Quantum Mechanics." In *Advances in Scientific Philosophy, Essays in Honor of Paul Weingartner*, ed. G. Schurz and G.J.W. Dorn, 215–29. Amsterdam: Rodopi.

Seckinelgin, H. 2017. *The Politics of Global AIDS: Institutionalization of Solidarity, Exclusion of Context*. Switzerland: Springer International Publishing.

Seckinelgin, H., and D. Paternotte. 2015. "'Lesbian and Gay Rights Are Human Rights': Multiple Globalizations and LGBTI Activism." In *The Ashgate Research Companion to Lesbian and Gay Activism*, ed. D. Paternotte and M. Tremblay. Abingdon: Routledge.

Sehon, S. 2011. "A Flawed Conception of Determinism in the Consequence Argument." *Analysis* 71 (1): 30–38

Sellars, W. S. 1962. "Philosophy and the Scientific Image of Man." In *Frontiers of Science and Philosophy*, ed. R. Colodny, 32–78. Pittsburgh: University of Pittsburgh Press.

"Shoesmith: 'I don't do blame'." 2011. *BBC Today*. Saturday, 28 May 2011 09:20 UK. http://news.bbc.co.uk/today/hi/today/newsid_9499000/9499424.stm.

Social Science Research Unit, UCL Institute of Education. 2016. "About the EPPI-Centre" [online]. Available at: https://eppi.ioe.ac.uk/cms/Default.aspx?tabid=63 [Accessed February 2018].

Spohn, Wolfgang. 1990. "Direct and Indirect Causes." *Topoi* 9: 125–45.

———. 2012. *Laws of Belief: Ranking Theory and its Philosophical Applications*. Oxford: Oxford University Press.

———. 2016. "How the Modalities Come to Inhere in the World." In *Erkenntnis*: 1–24.

The State of Missouri: An Introduction. 1998–2017. http://www.netstate.com/states/intro/mo_intro.htm [Accessed January 2019].

Strevens, M. 2012. "Ceteris Paribus Hedges: Causal Voodoo That Works." *Journal of Philosophy* 109:652–75.

Suarez, M. 2005. "The Semantic View, Empirical Adequacy, and Application." *Crítica: Revista Hispanoamericana de Filosofía* 37(109): 29–63.

Sutherland, W. J., L. V. Dicks, N. Ockendon, and R. K. Smith. 2015. "Conservation Evidence: Providing Evidence to Improve Practice." Available at: *What Works in Conservation* (2015), edited by William J. Sutherland, Lynn V. Dicks, Nancy Ockendon, and Rebecca K. Smith; http://www.conservationevidence.com/site/page?view=about [Accessed February 2018].

Thalos, M. 2013. *Without Hierarchy: The Scale Freedom of the Universe*. Oxford: Oxford University Press.

Tooley, M. 1987. *Causation: A Realist Approach*. Oxford: Clarendon Press.

Tugby, M. 2018. "Organic Powers." Ms, Durham University, Philosophy Department.

UK Department of Health. 2000. *An Organisation with a Memory: Report of an Expert Group on Learning from Adverse Events in the NHS*. London: The Stationery Office.

UNAIDS. 2016. "Maximising the Potential of a New HIV Prevention Method: PrEP" [online]. Available at: http://www.unaids.org/en/resources/presscentre/featurestories/2016/november/20161101_PrEP [Accessed February 2018].

van Fraassen, B. 1980. *The Scientific Image*. Oxford: Clarendon Press.

———. 1989. *Laws and Symmetry*. Oxford: Clarendon Press.

———. 2018. "Necessity and Possibility in Experience: A Reflection on Nancy Cartwright's *Nature's Capacities and Their Measurement*." Lecture presented in the symposium at UC Davis, organized by the Philosophy Department at UC Davis and the (San Francisco) Bay Area Philosophy of Science group, February 2018.

van Inwagen, P. 1983. *An Essay on Free Will*. Oxford: Clarendon Press.

Willimas, B. 1986. *Ethics and the Limits of Philosophy*. Cambridge: Harvard University Press.

Wimsatt, W. 1992. "Golden Generalities and Co-opted Anomalies: Haldane vs. Muller and the *Drosophila* Group on the Theory and Practice of Linkage Mapping." In *Fisher, Haldane, Muller, and Wright: Founders of the Modern Mathematical Theory of Evolution,* ed. S. Sarkar, 107–66. Dordrecht: Martinus Nijhoff.

Woody, A. I. 2015. "Re-orienting Discussions of Scientific Explanation: A Functional Perspective." *Studies in History and Philosophy of Science Part A* 52: 79–87.

Woolcock, M. 2016. "Using Mixed Methods in the Evaluation of Complex Projects." November, ms, World Bank, Harvard University.

Zwarenstein, M., S. Treweek, J. J. Gagnier, D. G. Altman, S. Tunis, B. Haynes, M. Gent, A. D. Oxman, and D. Moher. 2008. "Improving the Reporting of Pragmatic Trials: An Extension of the CONSORT Statement. *BMJ* 337: a2390.

Index

Adam (Biblical), 27
Adler, Alfred, 21
American Psychological Association, 40
analytic method, 30
    and force functions, 31–32
Anjum, Rani Lill, 106
Anscombe, G. E. M., 93, 100
approximate methods, 24
Aristotle, 4
Armstrong, David, 125, 127
artful modeling, 3–4. *See also* Nature: as artful modeler
    as basis for successful predictions, 19–20, 26
    as factual, 26–27
Augustus Caesar, 3
Austin, J. L., 104

Bacon, Francis, 93
Balls, Ed, 142, 144
Banerjee, Abhijit
    Poor Economics, 69
Barcan formulae, 47
Bayes nets axioms, 100
Beebee, Helen, 118, 131
Bellman equations, 36–37
Bentham, Jeremy, 93
best-system account (BSA), 116–17, 139–40
    and contingency, 123
    and determinism, 118–21, 123, 131
    and extent, 117–18
    and free will, 123
    and permissiveness, 118
    and potency, 123
    and reliability, 119, 123
    and violation of laws of nature, 122
Biannual International AIDS conferences, 62
big-picture differences, and local disagreements, 91
"big system," skepticism of, 92
Bird, Alexander, 41, 112, 127–32, 139
Bollhagen, Andrew, 77
Boole, George, 3
Brunel, Isambard, 3

Callender, Craig, 116
capacity account of laws, 136–38
    and contingency, 136
    and extent, 137
    and free will, 138
    and permissiveness, 136, 138
    and reliability, 138
carbon-14, 39–40
caricature Millikan theory (CMT), 31
Cartwright, Nancy, 112–15, 122, 133–35, 139
    "Causal Laws and Effective Strategies," 82
    The Dappled World, 104
    How the Laws of Physics Lie, 21, 30
    Nature's Capacities and Their Measurement, 32, 110
causal concepts, thick, 83
causal Markov condition, 39

causal powers, 32
causal process/chain, 143
causal relations, 82–83
causation
    Humean, 96
    and Principle CC, 96–97
causes, fixity of, 84
    and open future, 85, 89
    questions about, 91
    and reasons, 105, 108
Chang, Hasok, 23, 98
    "Active Scientific Knowledge," 6
'cheap heuristic,' 95
chess, possibilities in, 48, 88
Cohen, Jonathan, 116
commonsense empiricism, 81
Connelly, Peter, 142–43
Conservation Evidence (journal), 58, 58n77, 62, 65
consistency constraints, 97
context-centered approach, to policy, 57–58, 73
Coulomb's Law (CL), 31
Craver, Carl, 35, 135
Curie, Marie, 25–26, 106, 108

Darden, Lindley, 35, 135
Daston, Lorraine, x, 141
Davenport, Lee, 76
Davidson, Donald, 56
Deaton, Angus, 69–70
Democritus, 4
Descartes, René, 93
determinism, 85–86
dispositional essentialism (DE), 127–33
    and ceteris paribus laws, 129–30
    and determinism, 132
    and extent, 130
    and free will, 133
    and permissiveness, 129–30
    and reliability, 129, 131
Dretske, Fred, 125
Duflo, Esther
    Poor Economics, 69
Duhem, Pierre, ix, 6, 92, 102

Earman, John, 117–19
Einstein, Albert, 32
Elgin, Catherine, 101
empiricism, 23, 81
empiricist methodology, 23, 25–27
Epstein, Paul, 13, 15
evaluation studies, 40
evidence
    direct, 41–42
    indirect, 41
    as 3-place relation, 105
evidence-based policy (EBP) movement, 55
    context-centered approach, 55, 57–58, 62–64, 73
    intervention-centered approach, 55–62, 65–67, 69–73, 75
    problem of, 75
experiments, designing of, 48
"explanatory realism" (Hendry), 24

falsifiability, as practice, 7
Fischer, Florian, 6, 33–34, 43
Fletcher, Harvey, 7
Franklin, Melissa, 76
Frege, Gottlob, 3
Freud, Sigmund, 21
Frisch, Mathias, 103

Gadamer, Hans-Georg, 4
generalized Mackie formula (GMF), 65
Gigerenzer, Gerd, 95
Goldberg, Rube, 36, 60–61
Gonzalez, Juan Carlos, 4n1

Habermas, Jürgen, 4
Hardie, Jeremy, 65
Hart, H. L. A., 142–43
Haüy's Principle, 26, 106–07
Hendry, Robin, 24, 24n36
Holmes, Sherlock, 41
'Holmesian inference' (Bird), 41
Honoré, Tony, 142–43
human error
    person-centered approach, 144
    systems approach, 144

Index

Hume, David, 35, 39, 82–83, 93, 107, 135
Humean features, 12, 31n40, 35
Humean regularity account of laws, 116–25
Hume world, and modalities, 107

inductive inference
  and modalities, 106–07
  problems of, 106
Infeld, Leopold, 32
instrumentalism, 20
intervention-centered approach, to policy, 56–58, 65–67
  cause/effect in, 58
  conditions for effectiveness, 69
  and evidence, 66
  and Mackie claims, 66, 71–72
  markers and cautions for, 69–70, 75
  and pragmatic trials, 72
  problems of, 56, 59–62, 73
    concatenation, 61–62
    Donald-Davidson, 60–61
    long-view, 59–60
    and trial populations not well defined, 70–72

"Journals in Assessment, Evaluation, Measurement, Psychometrics, and Statistics" (APA), 40

Kant, Immanuel, 3
Knight, Margaret, 3
know-how, importance of, 19–20, 22–23, 25
Kremer, Michael, 42
Krueger, Lorenz, 103
Kuhn, Thomas, 14

Lamb, Willis, 97
Law of Composition (LoC), 31
Law of Gravity (LoG), 31
laws as relations among universals, 111–12, 125–27
  and extent, 126
  and modality, 127
  and permissiveness, 126–27
  and potency, 126
laws of nature, 29n39, 37, 111–12
  capacity account, 136–38
  and consequence argument, 123–25
  and contingency, ix–x, 111–12, 115–16, 139
  and determinism, 113–14
  and dispositional essentialism, 127–33
  as disposition/powers, 111–12, 114, 127–39
  extent, 113–14
  and free will, 113, 138–39
  Humean, 111–12, 114, 116–25, 131
  and modality, ix
  and permissiveness, 113–16
  potency, 113–14
  as relations among universals, 111–12, 125–27
  reliability, 113, 125–26, 139
  violation of, 139
Leibniz, Gottfried Wilhelm, 27
Leibniz's monads, 38
Lewis, David, 31n40, 47, 81, 116, 119, 121–22, 124–25, 127, 139, 139
  Counterfactuals, 116
  "Humean Supervenience Debugged," 116
  soft determinism, 121
  and violations of laws of nature, 121–22
Locke, John, 93
Loewer, Barry, 31n40

Machamer, Peter, 35, 135
Mackie, J. L., 65, 84–86
Mackie claims, 66
Marcus, Ruth Barcan, 47–48, 88
Marmodoro, Anna, 33n47
McKitrick, Jennifer, 40, 44
Menzies, Peter, 82
Merlussi, Pedro, ix, 86, 113
Miguel, Ted, 42
Mill, James, 93
Mill, John Stuart, 5, 31, 93, 98
Millikan, Robert, 7–11, 13, 15–16, 31, 37, 44, 49, 64, 73–74, 76, 84–85, 87

Mill-Ramsey-Lewis (MRL) view, 26–27, 38, 88
  critique of, 26
modalities, as part of the world, 107–08
Model-Apparatus Match (MAM), 74
Montuschi, Eleonora, 141
Morgan, Mary, 102
Mumford, Stephen, 105
Munro, Eileen, 141–43

natural and moral orders, as connected, 141
Nature. *See also* laws of nature
  as the artful bartender, 77–78
  as artful modeler, 3, 4n1, 5–7, 13, 23–24, 26–27, 38, 46, 49, 76, 85
  contingency in, 30
  endless possibilities in, 5, 19–20, 30, 50
  lack of proper laws in, 27, 37–38
  as open future, 81, 85
  possibilities in, 81, 88
Nature Conservancy, 46
  and artful modeling, 17–19
'Nature does it the way we do it,' 25, 30
Neurath, Otto, 81, 104
Newton's Law of Motion (NLM), 31–32
'no book to go by,' 13, 20
nomological machine, 29n39, 67, 82, 134
  and Trias powers, 67
Norton, John, 25, 106–07

O'Connor, John, 76
oil drop experiment, 7–13, 31, 64, 73–74, 84
  as complex practice, 9–10
  nature in, 11
  physical features in, 11
'only what actually happens,' 89

particularism, 104, 109
Peano, Giuseppe, 3
Pemberton, John, 68, 112–13, 133, 135, 139
philosophy of social technology, 55
physics, as falsifiable, 7
Plato, 4
policy effectiveness
  and arrangements, importance of, 61–62
  and context, 62–64
  and know-how/techné, 75–76
  predicting, 55–56
  and Trias powers, 56
Popper, Karl, 7, 21
possibilia, 47, 88
possibilities
  as endless, in Nature, 5, 19–20, 30, 50
  generating and fixing of, 48–49
  modal versus real, ix
possible worlds, 47
post hoc, ergo propter hoc fallacy, 40
powers, 29, 29n39, 84–85, 89. *See also* Trias powers
  as acting/influencing, 35–36, 43–44
  as capacities, 133, 135
  and conditionals, 43, 45
  "contribution" of, as problematic concept, 43
  evidence for, direct and indirect, 41–42
  as goal directed, 36, 37n54
  and how they combine, examples of, 50–54
  and possibilities, 48–49
  probabilistic, 38–39
PREP (Pre-exposure prophylaxis), 63
  in Kenya, 63–64, 70
principles, as true propositions, 20
Prior, Elizabeth, 43

quantum theory, 46–47, 87
Quine, Willard van Orman, 47

radium chloride, 106–07
Ramsey, Frank, 116
randomized control trial (RCT), 66
Reichenbach, Hans, 116
Reiss, Julian, 82
Roberts, Jean, 23n35
Robinson, Heath, 36
Rorty, Richard, 5
Russell, Bertrand, 3

Schiebe, Erhard, 109
Schoonmaker, Robert, 24n36
science
  as artful modeler, 6–7
  context-dependent propositions in, 13–16, 26

and convergence, 102
idealizations in, 101–03
as knowledge-how, ix, 5, 7, 20
lack of proper laws in, 23, 31
and particularism, 104, 109
rough-and-ready principles in, 25–26
symbolic representations in, ix, 6, 44
and system-specific models, 5, 12
scientific equations, as symbolic representations, 86
scientific image, 23, 26
scientific laws
    ceteris paribus (cp), 67–68
    extent of, 86
    Mill-Ramsey-Lewis (MRL) view of, 26–27, 38, 88
    permissiveness of, 86–87
scientific practice
    and analytic method, 29–32
    and powers, 29
scientific principles
    and falsifiability, 21
    as formulae, 30
    as not propositions, 30
    as not well formulated, 21
scientific realism, reconfiguring of, 20–22
Seckinelgin, Hakan, 62–63, 70
Sehon, Scott, 119–20, 131–32
    on violating laws of nature, 122
Sellars, Wilfrid, 11, 107
Shoesmith, Sharon, 142–44
Shomar, Towfic, 64
social systems, as mechanisms, 145
Spohn, Wolfgang, ix, 91–92, 104–110, 116
    and causation, 93–103, 105, 108
    "Direct and Indirect Causes," 100
    on general laws, 102
    and idealizations, 108
    inductive scheme, 106
    Laws of Belief, 94, 100
    and "limit of inquiry," 101
    'projected world' of, 93, 108
    relativization in, 94–95, 100
Stanford School, 91–92, 109
Stokes's Law (SL), 31–32
Stokes's principle, 13–17, 74

Strevens, Michael, 55–56, 67–68
    on scientific laws, ceteris paribus (cp), 67–68
Suarez, Mauricio, 7n6
supervenience, 12
Suppes, Patrick, 91, 93, 101
symbolic representations, in science, ix, 6, 44, 86
systems/mechanisms, in natural order, 144–45

Tarski, Alfred, 108
techné, 4–5
    versus episteme, 4
technology, as imitating nature, 4
To Err Is Human: Building a Safer Health System, 145
Tooley, Michael, 125
Trias powers, 6, 37, 37n54
    and contingency, 45–46
    and effects of the arrangement, 46
    features of, 44–45
    modes of acting, 46
    nature of, 46
    rules of combination, 46
Trias powers ontology, 30, 33–34, 38, 44–45, 56
    and analytic base, 33
    and evaluation studies, 42
Tugby, Matthew, 36
type-type reductionism, 12

UK's *Teenage Pregnancy Strategy*, 40–41

Vagnino, Richard, 77
Vandiver, Willard Duncan, 81
van Fraassen, Bas, ix, 81–82, 88–89, 94, 116
    on agency, 82–83
vector addition, 32, 46

Ward, Keith, 115
Waters, Alice, 3
What Works Centres, 55, 65
Wieten, Sarah, 68
Williams, Bernard, 83
Wimsatt, William, 122
Woody, Andrea, 6